525 Ways to be a Better Manager

SECOND EDITION

To Pauline, David and Peter

525 Ways to be a Better Manager

Second edition

Ron Coleman and Giles Barrie

Gower

Published by Gower Publishing Limited
Gower House
Croft Road
Aldershot
Hampshire GU11 3HR
England

Gower
Old Post Road
Brookfield
Vermont 05036
USA

Ron Coleman and Giles Barrie have asserted their rights under the Copyright, Designs and Patents Act 1988 to be identified as the authors of this work

British Library Cataloguing in Publication Data
Coleman, Ron
    525 ways to be a better manager. – 2nd ed.
    1. Management   2. Personnel management
    I. Title   II. Barrie, Giles
    658.4

    ISBN 0 566 07969 0

Library of Congress Cataloging-in-Publication Data
Coleman, Ron, 1941–
    525 ways to be a better manager / Ron Coleman and Giles Barrie. – 2nd ed.
       p.   cm.
    ISBN 0-566-07969-0 (hardcover)
    1. Management.   I. Barrie, Giles.   II. Title.
    HD31.C6116   1998
    658.4—dc21   98-24977
                                                                        CIP

Typeset in Palatino by Raven Typesetters, Chester and printed in Great Britain at the University Press, Cambridge.

Contents

Preface

Many years ago someone introduced me to the Peter Principle – that people continue to be promoted until they reach their level of incompetence – and I accepted it as a natural law. It certainly seemed to explain why there were so many ineffective managers. Some recent figures suggest that nearly 50 per cent of senior management appointments result in failure.

But I now realize that generally managers fail, not because they have been overpromoted, but because they haven't learned how to succeed. True, most have been promoted because they excelled in their previous job, but that should provide an ideal foundation, so what's the problem?

The problem is that there is so much to learn. Picking it up haphazardly is slow, wasteful and sometimes very painful, and it is not surprising that many fail. Enlightened employers worldwide understand this and graft on the new knowledge and skills systematically. It's quicker and more efficient, and can even be enjoyable.

Training is simply a way of learning from others' experience. Can you imagine doctors and dentists being allowed to treat us without rigorous training?

In revisiting my book eight years after the first edition was published I have to consider what is new in management. There is certainly plenty of new jargon. We have been re-engineered, down-sized, delayered, neurolinguistically programmed and empowered, but good managers have always done these things and only the words are new.

People are now sometimes referred to as human resources. I prefer to think of them as people but it is useful to be reminded that, like other resources, people should be expected to show a good return on investment.

The differences between well-run and badly run organizations are as clear as ever. Half of new businesses still fail within three years, generally because they have broken the same old basic rules by trying to expand too quickly or because they have not been firm enough with debtors.

Customers are ever more demanding. They expect to pay less and less for a higher quality of product. In competitive markets companies that fail to deliver surely die.

The pace has quickened. As more information travels electronically, at the speed of light, action is triggered more quickly. The car you order will be delivered within days and will incorporate improvements introduced since your test drive. The bad news is that the increased pace of business life has created so much anxiety that stress is now the cause of 60 per cent of sickness absence. So (back to basics) effective communication is ever more important to let everyone know what is happening. There are some interesting trends:

● Companies are now taking more care when recruiting. In particular there is much less reliance on interviewing as a selection method. Testing is much more common to ensure a good match with the person profile.

- The increasing use of technology should mean that businesses are more efficient. However, too often in the western world staffing costs remain high, resulting in a lack of competitiveness.
- Even now, people at work are being prevented from making a bigger contribution by their manager's unwillingness to delegate more. This seems to be due to their fear of not having enough to do, yet many of these managers are working excessive hours! Good delegators don't get fired, they get promoted!
- During a period when crime and, as far as we can tell, dishonesty have increased, managers have become more trusting. This has resulted in some huge corporate swindles and no doubt millions of other transgressions. Yet control as a management function is now frowned upon – we're told we should trust our staff. Let's not be foolish. Think of it as not being out of control. Call it monitoring or anything you like, but you do need to know what's going on.
- A very exciting development is the concept of self-directed teams. The team takes on the responsibility for managing itself. If each team member becomes a manager, then the proportion of managers to managed will change. Some forecasts predict that 1 in 4 of the workforce will be designated a manager by 2010 compared with 1 in 10 in 1990. With increased status comes increased responsibility. It is as important as ever to agree who is accountable for what.
- Perhaps the most obvious change is the continuing trend towards a more informal management style. Traditionally autocratic companies have changed their style. Managers are now mostly called by their first names, and they influence rather than just give instructions. They mix more freely with their teams. The old symbols of power and authority are fast disappearing.

Managers are more visible and the bad ones are therefore more easily identified. All good news.

How you will rapidly become a more successful manager

Invicta Training's 'Principles of Management' programme is probably the most successful management seminar in the UK. It has been attended by over 6000 managers from organizations including Coca-Cola, Rolls Royce, British Telecom, Motorola, Standard Life and Virgin – companies in different fields which realize that their most enduring competitive advantage is the quality of their management, and that all managers need the same core of knowledge and skills. That's what this book is about.

If you work for a non-trading organization don't be distracted by frequent references to suppliers, customers, sales and profit. Perhaps your 'customers' are taxpayers, donors or patients, and profit to you will mean making savings that will improve the service you can offer.

At Invicta, as we teach we learn, and those 6000 managers have shared with us what adds up to 90 000 years of experience as both managers and managed. You now also have an opportunity to share it.

Certain points in the text may remind you of things you used to do but have half forgotten. Managers, like drivers, can slip into bad habits.

Sometimes you will find similar pieces of advice under different headings. This is deliberate – the points have been marshalled under the main functions of management. It is a convenient way of presenting the material, but it doesn't reflect the day-to-day business of managing. For example, when running a meeting you're certainly delegating, making decisions and controlling – all at once. In other words, some overlap is inevitable.

Your Personal Action Plan

As you work through the book, make notes and underline

items of particular importance to you. Then, at the end of each chapter, list on the Personal Action Plan the things you must do.

Don't try to do everything immediately – have a top twenty list of priorities that deserve your special attention. Sometimes it will be difficult to break bad habits, so refer to the list daily. As you complete each task, cross it off and add further action points so that you always have a current top twenty.

And then . . .

There are no secrets of success. Management isn't a science, nor is it complicated. It is like any other job. Effective managers do certain things and if you apply these pieces of advice you will be an effective manager. And who knows where that might lead you?

Let me know how you get on.

Ron Coleman
Invicta Training Limited
240 Green Lane
New Eltham
London SE9 3TL

Introduction

What are you paid to do?

Before we look at each part of your job in detail, let's take an overview. Of course, you are paid to achieve results, but what results? Unfortunately most managers have only a vague idea; you need to know precisely. In a couple of sentences explain why your job exists.

To help you fulfil that purpose your company entrusts you with the necessary tools: money, people and material resources. The actual permutation is unique for every manager. Write down now what it is for you.

How are you responsible for your organization's money?

Are you required to operate within specified budgets? Do you have the authority to purchase? If so, what and up to what value? Do you forecast or control costs, direct or indirect – for example wastage, fuel, heating, lighting, security? Do you raise finance or commit your company to credit or leasing arrangements? Are you responsible for invoicing customers, receiving payments or chasing up outstanding accounts? Are you allowed to give discounts? If so, to what value? Must you grant it or do you have discretion? Do you have to deal with any outside organizations in connection with any of these responsibilities?

How are you responsible for your organization's people?

How many people are you accountable for – (a) directly, (b) through others? Do you decide their job content? Are you responsible for recruitment, selection, setting remuneration levels, job evaluation or job grading, designing or administering incentive schemes, terms and conditions of employment, training, industrial relations, health and safety, appraising, counselling, dealing with grievances, discipline, dismissals, termination and exit arrangements? Do you have to deal with any outside organizations in connection with any of these responsibilities?

How are you responsible for your organization's material resources?

Are you responsible for the acquisition, manufacture, storage, delivery, inspection, maintenance, repair, safekeeping or disposal of premises, plant, stock, components, vehicles, equipment or consumables? What control information do you have to gather, store, explain or pass to others? Do you have to deal with any outside organizations in connection with any of these responsibilities?

This exercise has helped you to define the extent of your managerial responsibilities. If you do not have a written job description, draft one and agree it with your manager (you will find an example on pp. 15–16). Discuss how your effectiveness is measured and the extent of your freedom to act without reference in each area. If you and your manager have not agreed what is required of you, how can you prove your worth?

What staff expect from their manager

List the ten qualities you would most hope to find in your immediate manager, and why. (Cover the list that follows the exercise.)

	Qualities	Why is each important to you?
1.		
2.		
3.		
4.		
5.		
6.		
7.		
8.		
9.		
10.		

You may like to compare your own list with those compiled by 6000 other managers. The qualities they mentioned most often are:

Ambitious
Enthusiastic
A clear communicator
Sets high standards
Firm and fair
An achiever
A good listener
Decisive
Supportive
Consistent
Open to new ideas

The lists made by 6000 people are uncannily similar, so it seems that most people have very similar expectations of their manager. The qualities most often quoted are the duet 'firm and fair'; apparently everyone wants to work for a strong manager. How do you match up? Why not ask your team?

In an interesting experiment in a badly performing school, the children were invited to assist with the recruitment of new teachers. They chose those who set high standards and were firm with pupils who misbehaved.

1

The art of managing people

Yes, it *is* an art. Computers cannot manage people because they are incapable of establishing a relationship.

Think of a time when you felt unhappy in your work. How did it affect your performance?

Research shows very clearly that people who are unhappy at work do their jobs less well, are more often absent and are more likely to leave. Your company will lose momentum and money unless you meet your team's main need – job satisfaction.

Help your team to enjoy their work by understanding what motivates each of them: recognition, achievement, money, security, involvement, good working conditions, personal development or promotion opportunities.

Create the right environment

First consider how you are satisfying the needs of your

1

team – how you make them look forward to coming to work each day.

1 Take special care when selecting staff. These decisions are among the most important you make at work. Match people very carefully to jobs – failure to do so is bound to cause dissatisfaction.

2 Remember that, like you, your staff are most effective when they enjoy their work. Review the content of each job regularly. Give people responsibility by having decisions made at the most junior level possible and extending authority when it is used well. But remember that you're always accountable for work you've delegated.

Ask yourself if everyone on your team has freedom to use their initiative.

3 Help people understand the importance of their work. Explain to them its purpose, the end product. They will know that their job is worthwhile when you give them feedback from customers or your own manager.

It's human nature to complain: you don't thank the postman or woman for every bill delivered, but perhaps you complain when one package arrives late. When you have good reports pass them on to your team and restore the balance.

4 Pay people fairly and competitively. It's not true that people who achieve a great deal and enjoy their work are happy in poorly-paid jobs. Money does motivate people. It pays the mortgage, buys the groceries and most of the things we enjoy. Most importantly, it demonstrates the value you, as a manager, put on a person's contribution.

Link financial rewards to individual performance whenever possible. Some contribute more than others – so pay them well. This isn't favouritism: competitors can find out your high-flyers' telephone numbers and tempt them with better pay: if you don't reward your best people, they'll leave.

Know what local firms and competitors pay and decide your place in the market. At one time 20 to 25 per cent of assembly-line workers at a car manufacturer were absent on Mondays and Fridays. They were highly paid but they were still unhappy because their jobs were tedious. Money on its own isn't a good enough motivator – you must satisfy all of your team's needs.

Use incentive schemes to reward individuals and teams for their contribution. People can't relate to global profit-share schemes – most of the operation is out of their hands and rewards from it are slow to be realized.

Incentives must be easily understood, designed to encourage appropriate behaviour and given immediately as a reward.

Introduce new schemes or new prizes; otherwise your people will begin to regard their Christmas turkey or their theatre tickets as a right, not a reward.

5 Provide the best working conditions you can afford. You invest heavily in your staff, so give them up-to-date equipment, civilized surroundings and good transport.

Work towards managers and staff sharing eating places, parking and toilet facilities.

6 Arrange regular performance reviews or meetings to discuss people's progress individually. Remember that you are their trainer and you develop their skills.

7 Set clear standards, that is, measurable minimum performance levels for all key tasks. These must be achieved by everyone. Also agree, with each individual, targets that will stretch them.

8 Measure everyone's contribution. If someone in your team argues that their job can't be measured, examine their job description with them and agree how each element of it should be monitored. Then ask them to record their progress.

9 Set high standards. Push for perfection. If you expect anything less, you'll disappoint your team and your customers. Employment agency Brook Street Bureau found that 62 per cent of people who leave clerical and secretarial jobs do so because they are underemployed – could some of this be because women are often put into jobs that don't tax their ability? Challenge is a big motivator: invite your team to agree to targets that are difficult, but attainable – your people need to be fully occupied.

10 Don't be too easily impressed. Make sure your standards are high enough to worry the competition.
Motorola's quality standards require fewer than six faults per million units, and they strive to do even better.

11 Never make promises you can't keep. It's unfair to mention rewards you can't deliver: don't ask your research team to work at night by promising a trip to Paris unless your directors have agreed.

12 Don't make your people feel insecure. If you are aggressive your team will make mistakes: because it is so damaging, aggressive management is disappearing.
Security is important, but don't promise a job for life – no company can forecast that far ahead. But never threaten

your people. Be honest about bad news and tell them what must be done to ease the situation, then train and push hard.

13 Don't keep secrets from your staff. You'll win respect if you are open with information. You give shareholders the figures – why not tell the people who have a bigger stake in the business by working for you all day, every day?

Secrets in business should be confined to the boardroom. Your people can legitimately obtain financial information on your company. If you withhold information people will assume there is a sinister reason – perhaps they are being underpaid or exploited. Let your team know how their company is doing.

14 Be polite and set a good example to your staff. Everyone must have a good impression of your team, so behave as you wish them to behave. Be punctual, loyal to the company, efficient and smart.

15 Measure absenteeism and staff turnover. These are the best indicators of job satisfaction. If staff are unhappy they are more likely to suffer genuine ill health. Research findings suggest that over 60 per cent of sickness absence is stress-related, so consider ways of reducing stress.

Monitor staff turnover. If the annual termination rate is above 10 per cent, unhappy staff are leaving. The best people go first – probably to your competitors. Don't blame the company or the competition – create the right environment and make your staff want to stay.

If staff turnover is disproportionately high in a particular job, study the job. Could it be made more interesting or challenging?

Your relationship with your team

Your team should respect you and feel relaxed with you. When you enter the room they should be pleased to see you.

16 Never behave as though you own your staff. You can't force people to work late or at weekends – everyone has an important life outside work. Developing greater efficiency and effectiveness will reduce the need for overtime working.

17 Treat people as individuals. Make allowances for their differences. Some people are creative; some work better with figures. Some people prefer to work alone; others in a team. Consider these characteristics when you recruit.

18 Always encourage teamwork and cooperation. Bring your people together, talk to them as a team – train people to do each other's jobs to increase flexibility and create interest and involvement.

People like to see their finished product. For years everyone at Freeman, Fox and Partners, from receptionists to engineers, was involved in the design and construction of the Humber Bridge. When it was completed the company paid for all its people to visit *their* bridge.

The cost of these gestures is small compared to the teamwork they promote.

19 Be consistent and don't have favourites. Don't allow friendships with team members outside work to affect relationships inside work. If a colleague, friend or sports partner misbehaves or performs poorly, treat them as you would anyone else.

Test people for further responsibility by delegating and setting projects. Make sure that everyone is given appropriate training to improve performance and develop as individuals.

20 Use incentives to unite the team. Company morale will be affected if, like a certain chemical company, you reward your sales team with a trip to Rio de Janeiro while the accounts department struggles to cope with the increase in business and wins no recognition. Friendly branch-versus-branch competition works well. Each team pulls together. Reward everyone who makes a contribution.

21 Talk directly to your people: don't drop hints about inadequacies – criticize constructively.

22 Treat everyone with respect, whatever their status. Never be patronizing towards people who are junior to, or less intelligent than, yourself. Your people need recognition, but don't praise too freely.

23 Behave naturally when you speak to more senior people. Tell your manager about team members who have done well – don't take credit for other people's work. Pass on good ideas, but don't present them as yours. Good ideas dry up for managers who steal the glory.

24 Don't encourage staff to talk to you about each other.

25 If there is conflict, bring the people together and talk the problem through.

26 Remember that you're only as good as your team. Don't let them down, don't be bossy. You need cooperation, not submission. Don't be moody, and never hold grudges.

27 Keep staffing levels lean so that everyone has to work hard. Very few companies have achieved adequate increases in efficiency from computerization and new technology. These savings will be more important as worldwide competition increases. When your team members do well, thank them for their extra efforts and praise them publicly. Give your team the leadership they deserve.

Whoever described management as a science had no experience of managing people. Human beings are complex and they are all different. Follow the advice in this chapter, but remember that, like any other art form, people management requires practice and a willingness to learn from mistakes.

Personal Action Plan

Managing people

Action	Target date	Achieved

2

How to recruit and select

You are as good as the sum total of your team. So to be successful you need to surround yourself with talented people. Many managers fear very able subordinates; the result is mediocre results and limited promotion prospects. In the UK six million people a year change jobs, and poor selection is certainly one of the main causes.

Organizations with high staff turnover soon earn a reputation as bad employers, and talented people who are in demand and have wide choice are not interested in joining them.

Whereas in the past selection mistakes could be easily rectified by dismissing the individual, tighter employment legislation has made this more difficult. Knowing how to pick winners is a key skill.

28 When anyone decides to leave your company, arrange a termination interview to discover their reasons. As their immediate manager you are probably too close to the situation, so it might be better if your manager or a colleague conducts the interview.

They must not be satisfied with false reasons for leaving but should seek the underlying cause.

29 Calculate the direct and indirect cost of losing and replacing staff. An experienced team member appreciates in value. Safeguard the investment by keeping your staff highly motivated.

30 When someone leaves, decide if you really need a replacement. By studying the job description and consulting the team, you may be able to reallocate the duties of the leaver and manage with one person fewer. That way you will achieve healthy savings and provide a greater challenge for your team. If you do need a person it might still be possible to redistribute tasks to increase efficiency and perhaps to prevent repetitive work always being given to the same person.

31 Don't promote people simply because they are good at their present job. Don't promote as a reward for loyal service – the aim must always be to appoint the most suitable person.

32 Give jobs realistic and helpful titles. Only use terms like director, executive, consultant and manager if they accurately reflect the job content.

The preliminaries

Of course, you are eager to fill the vacancy – but if you neglect the preliminaries you are almost certain to make mistakes that will be painful and expensive to correct.

33 Update or create a written job description for the vacancy. An example is shown on pp. 15–16. By calling together staff who will be working with the new person you may find ways to streamline the job. Perhaps it is time to introduce new technology.

34 Always create a person profile when recruiting, so that you don't overlook important features. This takes the form of an identikit picture in words detailing essential and desirable attributes (see specimen on pp. 17–19).

Be coldly analytical when preparing the profile.

On the day of the interview you may find someone's good points so appealing that you push their weaknesses to the back of your mind. This is known as the 'halo effect'.

Employing the wrong person is expensive and could seriously jeopardize the career of the recruit, who will probably have to be dismissed.

Be realistic – be sure that essentials *are* essential. Someone failing to match even one essential item will have to be rejected.

35 Be fair. If you are not clear on the law, take advice to avoid unlawful discrimination and never allow personal prejudices to affect your decision.

Companies that discriminate are the losers.

An organization that sells photocopiers had 200 sales representatives – all men; they had decided not to have female staff on the grounds that they weren't strong enough to carry copiers into demonstrations. Do you know *anyone* who can carry a photocopier? Within two years of being persuaded to recruit women, three of the top 20 representatives were female.

In many countries it is illegal to discriminate because of age. Rejecting someone because they are over 45 could mean missing a person who is mature, experienced and reaching their peak.

36 If the job is going to change, modify the person profile. Good health that is desirable now could become essential if a person is going to be switched to tiring outdoor duties.

Attracting suitable applicants

Now that you know exactly what you are looking for, you can start searching two areas. The person you need is either working for your organization already or they're somewhere else!

37 Recognize the advantages of appointing one of your own people. You will have a better opportunity to assess the person and they already have a good knowledge of your organization, products and systems.

It's good psychology to promote staff. Even companies that claim to have a policy of promoting from within too often bring in outsiders rather than train staff with potential.

38 Advertise vacancies on the noticeboard or in the company journal. Specify the essential and desirable attributes to avoid attracting people who are unsuitable.

Consider advertising inside and outside the company simultaneously to provide a wider choice and inject some competition.

39 Don't change the rules for internal applicants. The procedure must be the same as for everyone else. Internal applicants must match the person profile, prove themselves in an interview and complete any selection tests you may use.

Job Description

Date

Job title: Credit Controller
Company: Apex Civil Engineering Limited
Division: Finance
Responsible to (job title): Company Accountant
Main purpose: To obtain payment from customers with outstanding accounts. To keep credit levels within agreed limits.

Credit control	**Standard**
1. Maintain company-wide level of delinquency to within prescribed level.	Stage 1 – 5% of moving annual sales value Stage 2 – 2% of moving annual sales value Stage 3 – 1% of moving annual sales value Stage 4 – 0.6% of moving annual sales value

Customer contact	
2. Contact debtors at an appropriate level by telephone and obtain overdue payments whilst maintaining good customer relationships.	All debtors telephoned 7 days before due date. All stage 2–4 contacts at manager/director level Company customer-care standards observed at all times.
3. Visit customers to discuss payment difficulties and agree solutions.	Repeat business with prompt payment from 80% of ex stage 1–3 delinquents within 2 years.
4. Communicate in writing including stage letters 1–4 to expedite payment.	No errors in correspondence. All signed personally.

Records	
5. Maintain accurate records of all communications and transactions.	Zero defect records.

Progressing	
6. Pass stage 4 creditors to Company Accountant with a full written report of contacts and sequence of events.	Within one working day of missed stage 4 deadline.
7. Assist solicitors and respond to their requests for further related information.	Return telephone calls within one hour. Supply written/fax information within one working day.

continued

8. Appear at County Court hearings if required.	Successful injunctions.
9. Alert Sales Director to stage 4 creditors and 'do not deals' (DNDs).	Early alert at stage 2. 'DNDs' stage 3. Both within one working day.

External relationships

10. Take up credit references and searches on potential new customers.	Two trade references at manager/ director level and company search.
11. Give credit references within company policy.	Check authenticity of enquirer in accordance with company policy.

Other duties

12. Carry out other duties in the Accounts Department as requested.	Provide support as requested on at least 95% of requests.

Authority: To write off bad debts of up to £250. Strict adherence to credit procedure – no deviation other than with permission of Company Accountant.

Person Profile

Job title: Credit Controller   Date

This pro forma, based on the National Institute of Industrial Psychology seven-point plan, will help you compile an 'identikit picture' of the person you need to fill your vacancy. By your own definition *an applicant cannot be considered unless he/she matches all of your essential requirements.*

	Tick as appropriate	
	Essential	**Desirable**

A. Personal Characteristics

1. Physical. Special requirements in eyesight, hearing, height, strength, stamina, etc.; might a disabled person be suitable?

    Hearing and vision for telephone and computer operation
    Job could suit a disabled person — ✔ (Essential)

2. Personality. Attitudes, disposition, ability to work with others or work alone, cope with pressure, use initiative.

    Conscientious – must stick to the rules. Calm under pressure. Not easily fooled. Assertive – able to deal with aggressive customers. Tough-minded, determined. Good attention to detail. Content to work alone — ✔ (Essential)

3. Communicating skill. Oral, written, telephone manner etc.

    Fluency in oral and written communication — ✔ (Essential)
    Good listening skills — ✔ (Essential)
    Professional telephone skills — ✔ (Essential)

B. Attainments

1. Education. Examination passes, subjects, levels.

    English and Mathematics GCE 'O' Level or GCSE grade C — ✔ (Desirable)

2. Technical, commercial, professional qualifications, driving licence (groups).

    Membership of Institute of Credit Management by examination — ✔ (Desirable)

	Tick as appropriate	
	Essential	Desirable
3. Occupational training. Management, supervisory, accounts, purchasing, legal, sales, computer, customer care, credit control, first aid.		
Off-the-job training on:		
Debt recovery by telephone		✔
Customer care		✔
Company finance	✔	

C. Work Experience

1. Types of business, size of organization.

	Essential	Desirable
Civil engineering industry		✔
Large-company experience (£500 million turnover)		✔

2. Positions held. Level of seniority, length of service.

	Essential	Desirable
3 years' minimum successful credit control experience (or credit manager in a smaller company)	✔	

3. Specific knowledge and skills required.

	Essential	Desirable
Full working knowledge of credit control practice through to County Court	✔	
Detailed up-to-the-minute knowledge of legal framework pertaining to credit management	✔	
Skilful negotiator	✔	
Good organization/time management	✔	
Succinct report/letter-writing ability	✔	
Computer literate	✔	
Interpretation of financial statements	✔	

D. Special Aptitudes

Mechanical, languages, manual dexterity, facility with words, numeracy, creativity, problem solving etc.

	Essential	Desirable
Speed of thought – ability to grasp situations and spot solutions rapidly	✔	

	Tick as appropriate	
	Essential	Desirable
E. Circumstances		
Location in a particular area, willingness to travel, ability to stay away from home, work weekends, car owner etc.		
Live within convenient commuting distance	✔	
Able to travel within UK including occasional overnight stays	✔	
F. Other Requirements		
Longer-term company plan might involve credit controller working from home. Willingness to do so . . .		✔

40 If an internal applicant is unsuccessful, explain why. This can prevent rumours and bad feeling towards the person you select. Perhaps you should have prepared the person sooner and added necessary knowledge and skills in good time.

41 Encourage staff to introduce people they know for consideration. Some companies offer a financial incentive. This is cheap and convenient but there can be drawbacks. Could you dismiss your uncle or discipline your sister-in-law?

Beware of hidden discrimination. A large Midlands engineering company was found to be discriminating while recruiting only the friends of their employees, all of whom were white. They had to change their procedure.

Families and friends can be disruptive if they form cliques. If a powerful group of employees leaves your company to set up in business they may take your customers with them. Avoid this by putting a non-competition clause in contracts, but take legal advice on the wording.

42 Use your advertisement to screen out unsuitable people to avoid wasting your time and theirs.

43 Use appropriate media for recruitment advertising. Don't use expensive national press advertisements or professional head-hunters if cheaper alternatives are more suitable. Your trade press is usually the best way to reach people with experience in your industry, while the local press will attract people living within easy travelling distance.

44 Measure the effectiveness of your recruitment campaign by suitability, not quantity, of applicants. While you're wading through 800 replies the good people are being snapped up.

45 University placement officers and careers teachers will help you find suitable young people, so contact them and provide full information. Consider holding open evenings. Invite people who are interested in joining your organization. It is efficient and good public relations.

46 Recruitment agencies and job centres vary. The best will want to visit your business and work from the person profile. They will handle all screening and send only short-listed candidates for interviews.

The worst agencies just send CVs to you and hope you will pick someone for an interview. Check agencies who want your business, speak to their clients and find the best in your area or industry. Smaller agencies often try harder. Negotiate hard and make agencies work hard for their fees.

47 Consider people you short-listed recently for similar positions. Keep details of promising applicants on file. If they lack experience, invite them to reapply when they have gained it.

48 Make a direct approach to people you know are a good match for senior or specialist positions. If you use an experienced head-hunter expect to pay a fee of about 30 per cent of the annual salary.

Screening

If you have a number of applicants you will need to eliminate quickly those who are not in contention.

Telephone screening is particularly efficient. A yes/no quiz by telephone will disqualify anyone who lacks one or more essentials within a few minutes rather than after a lengthy interview.

49 Once the recruitment process is under way, keep it moving, as your good applicants will be talking to other employers, but do not be rushed into a decision. Acknowledge all applications within 24 hours even though you may need longer to decide whether to take the matter further.

50 Send a job description and company information with the application form. To reduce the risk of dishonesty the applicant must sign the application to confirm the facts and agree to instant dismissal if you subsequently discover false information.

51 Screen applicants against the person profile. You'll find out more from a completed application form than a curriculum vitae. CVs are often works of art prepared by professionals. They can mislead without actually telling lies.

52 For junior appointments do not assume that the applicant has written the application. It might be wise to check that they are literate.

Selection interviewing – preparation

According to research by University of Manchester Institute of Science and Technology, the selection interview is only 3 per cent more effective than pure chance in matching applicants to jobs. But that is probably more a reflection of the competence of managers as selection interviewers than a test of the technique.

A properly planned and skilfully conducted interview will help you to investigate in detail people who pass the initial screening.

53 Revisit the person profile – in particular, previous experience required. List 8–10 behavioural questions to ask every candidate to tell you how they behaved in various situations in previous jobs – how they dealt with a crisis, introduced a new system, resolved a problem and so on. You will want specific examples.

54 Study application forms carefully and decide what needs further investigation. Find out why applicants left previous jobs: you will often need to probe for the truth and clarify vague details.

55 Allow enough time for each interview and give yourself thinking time between candidates to write up your notes. Do not allow candidates to gather in the waiting room. It can make people feel uncomfortable and give a poor impression of your organizing ability.

56 Interview where you cannot be overheard, and prevent interruptions. The environment is important – neither you nor the interviewee should be distracted.

57 Give your receptionist a list of candidates with their appointment times. You might gain a useful insight into people's suitability by asking your receptionist for their impression of the candidates. People act more naturally when they are relaxed, so the receptionist might have observed something useful.

58 If you have a large number of applicants, take a Polaroid photograph of each and pin it to the interview notes. This will help you recall faces after a full day of interviewing.

59 Remember the importance of candidates having a good impression of the company, and explain this to your staff. Never looked bored or tired even if you are.

Selection interviewing – technique

When you meet applicants you will be tempted to rely on your skill as a judge of people, but instinct is no substitute for a probing interview.

60 Don't rely on instinct or first impressions. If you have difficulty being objective when judging others, keep reminding yourself of the person profile.

Instant likes and dislikes are often based on the applicant's resemblance to someone. Beware of stereotyping candidates 'all … are …'. Interviewing is not that simple.

61 Put applicants at ease. People are always nervous at interviews. By helping them relax you'll be better able to assess their suitability.

62 Explain the job but don't oversell it. Tell the candidate about any drawbacks. Sales managers often have difficulty with this: they may instinctively regard any face-to-face meeting as an opportunity to persuade people.

Make sure you have to hand any information or literature you might need during the interview.

63 Control the interview and keep it on course. After explaining the job and answering any questions, ask the candidate to reaffirm their interest. Then don't do more than 25 per cent of the talking.

64 Ask questions that help you visualize the applicant in the job. How would you deal with ...? Suppose...? What if...?

65 Test the knowledge the candidate claims to possess. 'What stock-turn figure would you expect in this kind of store?' 'What percentage of sales would marketing normally cost in this industry?'

66 Be careful when considering people who work for a competitor and don't take their knowledge and skills for granted. Don't give away any secrets – they could be spying on your company.

Remember that someone willing to bring business from their present employer might take your business away in the future.

67 Listen carefully to everything the candidate says and for inflections in their voice which often reveal emotions and attitudes beyond what they say. Make brief notes during the interview but arrange the seating so that the interviewee cannot see what you are writing.

Don't snatch up your pen if the candidate says something that might damage their chances – you might shatter their confidence. Hold the point in your mind and note it down a couple of minutes later, but do investigate the doubtful area fully.

Be straightforward, and explore any doubts you have straight away. You need to be certain that the person fully matches the person profile essentials, and has as many desirable attributes as possible.

The interview has to be searching. It is much more than a chat. There is so much at stake, and mistakes are always expensive.

68 Facial expressions and body movements will also give useful clues. Sudden movements can indicate unease – perhaps you are touching on a subject you need to investigate.

69 Encourage the candidate to talk, but don't prompt. 'This job would mean an early start. Can I take it that you would be happy to get up at 4.30 every morning?' is no use. 'When did you last get up at 4.30?' would be more revealing.

70 Don't judge people on their interviewing ability. Extroverts are better at projecting themselves and you might warm to them. Sometimes this is right for the job, sometimes it isn't. To work alone, the right person would probably be reserved.

Beware of people who have become more skilful interviewees through plenty of practice – they might anticipate questions, detect unintentional signals from you, ask excellent questions and mislead without actually lying.

The ideal person may have very little experience of being interviewed.

71 If it becomes clear during the interview that a person is not suited to the job, tell them. You may feel awkward but it's time-wasting and cowardly to deceive applicants, and you could harm your company's image by sending them away feeling confident and then disappointing them with a letter of refusal or, even worse, not contacting them at all.

Winners and losers

Staff selection is always a gamble to some extent, but do study the form carefully and leave as little as possible to chance. The best guide you have to how people will behave in future is how they have behaved in the past. Invest in winners.

72 Beware of selecting someone who is overqualified unless the job is going to grow soon. People who are underemployed will become bored and leave.

73 Be on your guard against applicants who are looking for a short stay while they seek a more permanent position elsewhere. You might invest three months' training in someone and lose them before they reach an acceptable performance level. Express your doubts on this point honestly.

74 Beware of applicants who have frequently moved from employer to employer. They'll probably blame their previous managers and in 15 months be blaming you too. You don't want people who lack integrity in your team.

75 Consider whether the applicant will be compatible with other members of your team. Before you make a decision, invite him/her to spend a half-day in the department and ask for the team's views.

76 Remember that people whose careers show a record of achievement and progress are likely to continue to succeed. Be wary of applicants who claim to be unlucky, however credible their explanations.

77 Always resist the temptation to select the best of a bad bunch. Selecting someone you know isn't right for the job almost guarantees that you'll have to repeat the whole process before long. The team would prefer to work harder until you find the right person.

78 If there are a number of suitable applicants, use selection tests rather than more interviews to help you identify the best.

79 Don't be rushed into a decision – especially by an eager applicant. When you have made your decision, think again. If your manager complains that recruitment is costing too much or taking too long, remind him/her of the cost of hiring the wrong person.

Selection testing

Suitable applicants will need to demonstrate their eligibility. Most experienced managers have at some time made the mistake of accepting an applicant's assurances that they have the knowledge and skill for the post and regretted it later. You must be more cautious.

80 Use tests to measure skills. Diagnosing the fault in a television set, a typing test, calculating discounts, by conducting the interview in a foreign language if fluency is needed, making sure a person gives the correct change, giving them an in-tray exercise, an accompanied drive – these are examples. Capable applicants will be happy to demonstrate their ability.

81 When filling senior or key positions use well-validated tests to explore aptitude, intelligence and personality.

This will probably involve specialists from outside the business who will design a battery of appropriate tests called an assessment centre.

82 Don't keep short-listed candidates waiting for a decision – you'll lose them. Bring them back to the company and test them further.

Final checks

If there is still someone under consideration you are fortunate, but even now you are not ready to make a job offer.

If there is no potential candidate left you will have to start again. Inconvenient though it may be, it's better than appointing the wrong person.

83 Where good health is important, make job offers conditional on a medical examination. Arrange for the selected candidate to be examined by your company doctor.

Do not discriminate on the basis of disability: explore ways of enabling disabled people to do the job.

84 Always ask for documentary proof of professional and academic qualifications. Consider how rarely you have been asked for proof of these and you'll realize why so many people make false claims.

This includes the careful checking of driving licences.

85 Always check references. Telephone the successful candidate's two most recent immediate managers and ask for confirmation of what you've been told. 'I understand he headed a department of 12 people for three years and consistently achieved objectives and always operated within budgets.' This can lead to a wider discussion, but ask for facts rather than opinions. When told 'we don't give references on the telephone', persist and explain that you would appreciate confirmation of a few facts, and most managers will oblige. Written references are usually bland and of little use, but if that's all you have, include them in your decision-making process.

The total cost of losing and replacing even a junior employee will be thousands of pounds, including the many hidden costs. The importance of recruitment and careful selection often isn't recognized. Selecting a junior manager in their mid-twenties who stays with your organization until retirement could represent an investment of three-quarters of a million pounds. If your company was investing that amount in machinery or property there would be board meetings and in-depth research. But until the importance of recruitment is properly understood, it's up to you to recruit the staff you deserve by always finding a good match for the job. No decision in business is more important to you.

Personal Action Plan

Recruitment and selection

Action	Target date	Achieved

3

How to plan

As a director or senior manager you are concerned with the setting of company-wide, long-term objectives – the strategy. If you are a middle manager you will be agreeing monthly and annual plans and forecasts. If you are a junior manager you will be planning in the short term, dealing in days, hours or sometimes from minute to minute.

These days, fewer companies have planning departments: planning is a function of line management. Strategy can't be carved in granite and managers at all levels must be more flexible as companies react to external forces.

Companies that don't recognize the need to change can slip into rapid decline, and managing change can be the difference between a successful and unsuccessful management team.

86 Ask your manager to inform you of corporate plans. This will help you better appreciate the role you'll play.

87 Discuss and agree with your manager measurable performance objectives that will test your effectiveness. Vague targets are useless. If your manager is not convinced of the need for management by objectives, you must propose the objectives yourself and suggest how your performance should be measured.

88 Never agree to objectives that you believe are unachievable. Instead you must express your doubts firmly and reach agreement. Don't be intimidated by your manager's seniority – speak up.

89 Have an up-to-date plan for each of your objectives detailing key tasks and indicating by when they have to be completed.

90 Have planning meetings with other managers to ensure continuity. Draw up an agenda and achieve agreement.

91 Manage change skilfully. Be ready for people to be afraid or suspicious of new situations: 'But we've always done it that way'; 'It will never work' are common protests.

Before people let go of old methods they may be depressed and frustrated, but don't abandon your plan. Reassure and explain the need for change, and keep people informed: few situations are more worrying than silence.

Once people have tested and understood your ideas, they'll see how change leads to growth. Involve your team in the planning of change and they will become excited by it. People who work for progressive companies are proud of being ahead of the field.

Older people tend to take longer to adapt to change and may need counselling to accept innovation.

92 Read the financial and trade press. In Japan most of the working population know about their industry and their competition through avid reading.

Delegate reading to your team and ask them to highlight important articles and report news to you.

You need private thinking time. Close your door if you don't want to be disturbed. Study performance figures – draw graphs, bar charts and pie charts. What are the figures trying to tell you?

93 Consult when planning. Remember that junior people have useful knowledge that you need. Those in direct contact with customers are a good source of information.

94 Don't *tell* people what they have to achieve – win their support by agreeing objectives, and persuade if necessary. Set honest targets and avoid business politics.

An insecure sales manager who predicts mediocre results won't be congratulated when sales records are broken if the production department can't meet demands or there are not enough vehicles to transport the goods.

The plan will not work unless you consult honestly and regularly.

95 Set clear objectives. It's no use simply asking staff to do their best. They, like you, need objectives to measure their performance. Make objectives demanding. Ask your team what they can achieve and most will be optimistic; impose objectives and they will resist, resenting your patronizing attitude, however reasonable the targets.

96 Don't change the rules. If, having agreed objectives with your team, you then increase targets, you will undermine their trust in you.

97 Planning involves note-taking. Keep your notes, including calculations, for future reference. Your manager will probably question you closely on matters you have forgotten.

Long-term planning

If your aim is to reach the top you must learn to take a long-term view. Focusing on the destination is not enough. You must plan the route.

98 Pass information and suggestions to your manager to help with strategic planning. Study market trends – senior management will see ways to keep ahead of the competition, perhaps by diversifying, acquisition, or through organic growth.

British American Tobacco became BAT Industries and moved away from the tobacco market. They bought Eagle Star Insurance, Allied Dunbar, Wiggins Teape, Dollond & Aitchison and other companies, but like many conglomerates have regrouped and concentrated on their core activity – tobacco. Virgin, on the other hand, continue to move into new markets.

99 Encourage creativity, using brainstorming sessions to produce strategic planning ideas. Have a brief warm-up, perhaps with an amusing subject, quickly list ideas on a flipchart, then ask: 'What new markets should the company look at?' 'How could we improve our service to customers?'

Ask for *any* ideas and don't allow people to criticize suggestions. Building upon ideas is more useful than rejecting them and will encourage your team to be confident and adventurous in their thinking. Brainstorming provides more workable suggestions than conventional discussion.

Your role is to be a catalyst to encourage and to draw people out – especially the quieter members of the group.

Explain lateral thinking and the importance of always looking for better customer-care techniques. Nashua Corporation has sold more of its original product – paper – by entering the photocopier and computer supplies markets.

Everyone in your team is creative – it's up to you to draw out their ideas.

100 Involve your team. Full consultation is possible even in very large organizations. Unilever has trading interests in most countries but is prepared to take time to give people at all levels the opportunity to participate. In this way Unilever is assured of far more commitment than is achieved in companies whose head office dictates plans through issued pronouncements.

101 Study past performances. Base plans on fact, not guesswork. Plan to make better use of resources every year. If you plan company growth of 20 per cent you should not need 20 per cent more people or 20 per cent more equipment – growth should help you take advantage of economies of scale.

102 Start the business plan with a sales forecast; that will provide the basis for other departmental plans and indicate whether you need further accounts staff, a new branch, extra training and so on.

Base sales forecasts on past performance and thorough research. Monitor trends, seasonal variations and any identifiable cycle in your industry – only predict a dramatic improvement in sales if you have good reason. Forecasts must be realistic.

103 Plan backwards from each forecast and decide what needs to happen stage by stage. Use critical path analysis (CPA). Construction managers have flow charts that show when a site will be cleared, when foundations will be laid, when materials will arrive, with some jobs carrying on simultaneously: bricks can be delivered while the site is cleared, but can't be used until the foundations are complete, so bricklayers must be called in at the right time. CPA works in the same way for coordinating a new product, for design, from production to sales, moving office, opening a new branch, reducing waste and maintaining work schedules.

104 Systematically review and update long-term plans. Devise methods to sell more products to existing customers and experiment with ways to win new customers. Investigate buying motives and how they are changing.

105 Senior managers must set clear company-wide standards: telephones must be answered before the third ring, correspondence must be answered within 24 hours, delivery vehicles must be washed daily. These are too important to leave to individuals, and managers at all levels must rigorously enforce standards.

106 Communicate the plan, and keep the team informed of the organization's objectives. Many companies publish mission statements which detail the main aims of the business so that everyone identifies with them.

Don't imagine that your staff are not interested or that they will not understand: presenting information clearly at departmental meetings will win their commitment and develop team work.

107 Have contingency plans. Don't be pessimistic, but do allow for hiccups – a crisis is much worse if you haven't anticipated its possibility and the consequences. Ask yourself, 'What would we do if a particular supplier went on strike?' 'What would we do if there was a long power cut?' If the worst happens, learn from the experience so that next time you will have a tested plan.

108 If your company is involved in a merger or acquisition explain that everyone has to adapt. Obtain full details as soon as possible to prevent anxiety and as far as possible consult on ways to achieve maximum benefit. Talk with everyone concerned rather than send written announcements.

Short-term planning

Only by becoming skilled as a short-term planner will you earn the promotion that will put you in control of the organization's future.

109 Have a short-term plan for this month, this week, today.

110 Use a daily action checklist. Keep an up-to-date 'to do' list, revise it at the end of each day and enjoy crossing items off.

111 Make time to think: don't be worried if staff see you scribbling or looking into space. A manager can be as productive thinking as when 'walking the job' or attending meetings.

112 Decide your priorities: what's urgent, what's important. A task isn't urgent because you enjoy it, so work hard at parts of your job you don't like. As you improve at them you'll learn to like them more.

113 Use a diary and, if appropriate, a wall planner. Talk to well-organized colleagues about time-management systems. If you have a secretary, synchronize diaries every morning.

114 Don't schedule meetings, interviews or visits too tightly. Don't keep your directors waiting for an annual report or keep a new recruit waiting for an induction interview because you are hurrying back from an exhibition.

115 Circulate agendas in advance to save time in meetings.

116 If your work piles up, go to work an hour early and enjoy beating the traffic, feel fresher and accomplish in that one hour the work that would normally take three, before everyone else arrives. Try to avoid taking work home.

Why do so many managers believe they should always appear busy? You would not set off on a journey without sitting down and carefully planning your route and making a list of what you need. Don't give planning at work any less attention – it is time well invested.

Personal Action Plan

Planning

Action	Target date	Achieved

4

How to organize

Once you and your team are clear about what has to be achieved, the challenge is to achieve it. You have considered your role by detailing your responsibility for the company's people, money and material resources – these are the tools with which you will achieve your objectives.

To maximize these resources, which are all precious and all costs, you need organizing skill. Your aim is to achieve a good return on your company's investment in you and everything that you manage.

If you believe you are under-resourced, discuss the problem urgently with your manager. You must present a powerful, logical case.

117 Remember, resources are scarce: an extra person for you might deprive another department of an important team member. If your manager disagrees and says you don't need an extra person, a new computer module or a larger budget, they must explain how you could manage more efficiently. Don't allow your manager to brush you aside – the satisfactory resolution to what you see as a real problem is essential to your success.

118 Have telephone calls and unexpected visitors screened so that you deal only with important matters. You're paid to be a manager, not a receptionist.

119 Ask your staff for suggestions to improve efficiency. Act on good ideas and give your people credit for their suggestions. Lucas Industries and Ford achieve huge savings through productive suggestion schemes with rewards – cash or even holidays. Asking people to post letters in a suggestion box does not produce the best ideas: invite people to explain their proposals.
Disneyland was the idea of a junior Disney employee.

120 Help your people increase their efficiency. Your sales people want to be selling, not doing paperwork, so keep their administration simple and explain why you need accurate information on time. Good organization depends upon everyone understanding what is required and why.

121 When you go out, tell people how you can be contacted or telephone the office regularly.

122 Make it clear who is responsible for what when you are away. Ensure continuity and assess potential managers by delegating parts of your job. If you test people it's unlikely they'll be overpromoted.

123 Win a reputation for 'following up'. When colleagues and team members agree to do things, or to give you information by an agreed date, put pressure on them if they seem to be letting you down. Always agree a 'by when' date.

Organizing your team

Your team is like a sports team. You must select people carefully and put them in the right positions. They need to function as a team and outperform the competition.

124 Produce an organization chart showing who reports to whom, distribute copies and keep it up to date.

Matrix management is a more complex system by which people report to different managers for various parts of the job. Everyone must know to whom and for whom they are responsible. They should know who appraises, disciplines, trains and, if necessary, who should dismiss each individual. In recent years, organization charts have tended to be broader based and the number of levels reduced. Toyota and other successful companies have just five levels. Have only as many immediate subordinates as you can manage, which is not normally more than 12.

125 Agree a written job description (see example on pp. 15–16) with each team member and be sure to update it at performance appraisal interviews. If you have a matrix structure, then agree a separate job description for each role.

126 Don't imagine that people will restrict themselves to a narrow interpretation of their job because of the chart or a job description. Poor team spirit is caused by bad leadership, not good organization.

127 Give people freedom to act within clear limits. If they are not clear about their authority they will make mistakes until you stop them or they will refer every decision to you, interrupting your work.

128 Insist on choosing your immediate subordinates. If you have human resources specialists, arrange for them to handle recruitment advertising, screening and preliminary interviews. Welcome their advice but make the final decision yourself.

Keep staffing levels lean. Your customer has to pay for any inefficiency and that can make your company uncompetitive. IBM and many other large corporations have improved their competitiveness through large staff reductions. Do not expect customers to subsidize inefficiency.

129 Identify training needs and arrange for appropriate management and staff training to keep everyone's knowledge and skill level up to the requirements of the job.

130 Increase the responsibilities and decision-making authority of people who can cope with a greater challenge. Most people can contribute far more than their managers will allow.

Delegate decision making whenever possible. Apart from freeing you to manage, it will enable you to recruit higher-calibre staff into junior positions.

Managing your time

Your time is different from other resources – the terms can't be changed. Every manager is a year older than 12 months ago and there are still 24 hours in a day. You can usually correct a mistake made with other resources but a wasted hour is lost for ever. Think of a senior manager who impresses you. Are they always under pressure and dashing from place to place? Of course not. They are organized.

131 Calculate the cost to your organization of an hour of your time and be determined to give good value. As a manager you are paid to plan, organize, control and provide leadership, and the more senior you are the more of your time should be spent on these activities.

132 Log your time over at least ten working days. Guessing is pointless, so measure in 15-minute segments how you spend each day: Tuesday, week 2, telephone 2 hours, meetings I chaired $4\frac{1}{2}$ hours, reading and writing 1 hour, travelling 1 hour, meetings I attended 1 hour, planning and thinking $\frac{1}{2}$ hour, interruptions $\frac{1}{2}$ hour.

Draw a pie chart to illustrate how you spend your time during the period.

133 Now remind yourself of your key objectives and consider whether you are using your time as well as possible. Three questions will help you achieve dramatic time savings:

1. Do I do jobs that needn't be done at all?
2. What could I delegate?
3. Could the jobs I have to do be done more efficiently?

The 6000 managers who have asked these questions of themselves on Invicta Training programmes have found ways of saving an average of eight hours per week. Question 2 usually offers the greatest scope.

134 Identify now three tasks that you will delegate to members of your team. If you believe this doesn't apply to you, think hard about parts of your work that you are especially good at or enjoy; you might find that this is why you haven't relinquished them.

135 Don't be persuaded by your manager or colleagues that you ought to be working very long hours and that you should not go home at the official closing time.

Many managers work excessive hours because they are badly organized. Some are afraid to delegate, believing that they should be busy (perhaps someone should invent a new name for 'business'!).

136 Insist on brief memos and reports which show recommendations first. Consider ways of streamlining reporting systems. Submit reports to your manager on time.

137 Before making telephone calls list the points you need to cover and encourage others to be brief.

138 In meetings you chair be firm and remind people to come with ready-formed ideas. Could you sometimes send a deputy to meetings instead of attending yourself?

139 If you travel during work, consider using public transport to make time for reading, writing and thinking.

140 Manage with an open door, but don't encourage casual visitors. Tell people if they have called at an inconvenient time. Leave your door open when you are available for visitors, close it when you must not be disturbed. Ask people to make an appointment or come back later. If you work in an open-plan office you will need to be even stricter.

141 Don't make short-stay visitors too comfortable – walk towards them as they enter and don't automatically offer them a seat or a coffee.

Talk about business and use direct questions to move away from small talk: 'So, Jack, why can't we open the Oxford branch by the November deadline?'

142 However busy you are, set a good example by keeping your office tidy. If you were unable to come to work could someone else easily take over?

143 Take your full holiday entitlement and get enough rest to stay healthy. In January every year Mark McCormack, founder of the International Management Group, crosses out weeks in his diary for holidays – he has achieved this lifestyle by employing talented people and delegating as much as possible.

Don't be impressed by less able managers who boast that they haven't had time for a holiday for years.

Managing the company's money

There are many similarities between organizing the finances in business and running a household. It is easy to overspend; the skill is to spend wisely and live within your means.

144 Operate within agreed budgets. Overspending by just 3 or 4 per cent might not seem serious, but if every manager did so it could mean the difference between profit and loss.

145 Remember that increased turnover doesn't necessarily mean bigger profits. The offer of an enormous order might not be the good news it appears to be. Calculate the costs carefully and sleep on it before making a decision – perhaps to negotiate more favourable terms.

146 Spend the company's money as if it's your own. Encourage your team to moderate their expenses and keep heating, lighting, fax and telephone costs down.

Take advantage of low offers. When buying don't automatically select the cheapest (or the most expensive) alternative and always press for discount. Negotiate hard with suppliers, push for concessions and deferred payment whenever possible.

Organizing material resources

You need to be as careful in selecting premises, vehicles, equipment and stock as in choosing staff. That way you can give the best possible value to your customers.

147 Equip your people properly. Don't economize with cheap equipment, materials and training if work will suffer. Investigate the benefits of purchase, leasing, rental and contract hire of equipment.

Marks and Spencer take good care of their staff and provide excellent working conditions: their reputation as an enlightened employer enables them to attract and retain high-calibre staff.

The cost of good working conditions is repaid by a highly motivated, productive workforce.

148 Have staff trained to help them make full use of equipment – do you and your team use your modern telephone system to best advantage?

149 Optimize use of equipment through preventive maintenance. Have vehicles and all machinery serviced according to manufacturers' recommendations – don't wait for faults to develop. Breakdowns and all waste and inefficiency have to be paid for by the customer.

Improving systems

Continually be on the lookout for ways of improving efficiency, and that means simplifying systems. Keep reminding yourself of your objectives.

150 Help your team appreciate the importance of sound administration. Everyone must understand how information flows within the organization and why it is needed.

Take full advantage of new technology. If you're not an expert, seek independent, specialist advice on equipment or you could waste money.

151 Once a year assemble your team and together challenge every standard document you use in the department. If any documents are not making a useful contribution, eliminate them.

152 Study the layout of the work area in relation to the flow of work. How paper moves around the office is often ignored – people might be positioned according to how a supplier unloaded the office furniture.

Remember that efficiency is doing things right, and effectiveness is doing the right things. You need to be efficient and effective. As a well-organized manager you will control your career rather than be swept along like some disorganized colleagues.

Personal Action Plan

Organizing

Action	Target date	Achieved

5

How to maintain control

A standard is the minimum level of performance you will accept. With ever greater emphasis on quality the standard required is 100 per cent. Monitor performance to ensure that standards are being maintained. Invite the team to monitor their own performance. Self-managed teams need the authority to take action; they also need to be firm with colleagues who are not making a satisfactory contribution. Encourage openness. If there is a problem it must be discussed frankly and a solution found.

You are clear about the plan and you are skilfully organizing your resources to achieve it. Control is the means by which you monitor actual performance to check that everything is happening as it should.

This is not control in the old-fashioned sense of restriction and prevention – the aim is to help everyone take on as much responsibility as possible. The important thing is not to be out of control! You need:

(i)   clear, unequivocal standards of performance detailing the minimum quality and quantity of work that you will accept;

(ii) a reporting system that helps you monitor each team member's performance.

You need accurate, relevant information early enough to enable you to correct any variation before it becomes serious.

153 Measure your performance against your objectives. Twenty years ago, even in the most successful businesses, managers at review meetings would discuss trading results for the month before last, but today this time-lapse would send the company out of control.

Modern IT systems transfer information at the speed of light and head offices of large retailers now know how much money they're taking minute by minute in branches around the country.

154 If you are not achieving your objectives don't blame other people, your competitors, the economy, trade unions or the value of the pound. Accept responsibility, put together a plan to get back on course, and talk it through with your manager.

155 Don't generate constant pressure – you'll damage your team's health and your own. If your style is overbearing or threatening you will increase absenteeism and staff turnover.

People must know what you expect. Capable people will leave if there are frequent misunderstandings or a lack of continuity, so stay in close contact with all your staff.

156 Don't manage from behind a closed door. 'Walk the job' and stay informed but don't expect to find problems. Do not ask 'Are there any problems?' 'How are things going?' or 'Is everything all right?' are far better openings. Generally, ask people specific questions that you want them to be considering for themselves: 'How many orders have we had this morning?' 'Have we received the ABC cheque yet?'

157 Don't talk to people only when things go wrong. Be fair, and remember to thank them when things go well – which is most of the time.

158 Be honest if you don't like something – don't ignore problems to keep the peace; insist on your staff paying careful attention to small details.

159 Don't shout, swear or lose your temper. Control begins with self-control. Your staff will follow your lead if you are polite and assertive. Explain to them the damage caused by aggressive behaviour inside and outside the business. Learn how to disagree agreeably – raising your voice will not make you more persuasive.

160 Act quickly and decisively, never hastily, to solve problems. Measure twice, cut once.

161 Reduce all types of waste. Control costs and prevent abuses such as excessive claims for mileage, long telephone calls, private calls and unnecessary mail. A 2°C reduction in the heating setting could save a great deal of money without making people uncomfortable.

162 Always operate within company policy. If you disagree with a policy, present a powerful case to have it changed; in the meantime follow the policy laid down.

163 Ask your own manager not to give instructions to your staff. If your manager persists in bypassing you, you will lose control. Explain that only you should delegate to your team, to avoid confusion.

164 Arrive punctually for meetings. If you are chairing, start business immediately and discourage lateness. Involve everyone and keep discussion to the point. Circulate action minutes immediately, indicating who has agreed to do what and by when, then follow up to ensure that the action is taken.

165 To keep meetings brief, schedule them immediately before lunch and don't provide refreshments; or perhaps provide sandwiches and have a working lunch. Meetings at the end of the day are more likely to be brief, but don't expect people to be at their best.

166 If you attend meetings that are chaired badly by another manager tell them tactfully. Even if it is your own manager explain the problem privately. Poorly controlled meetings waste time.

Financial control

Don't leave control of money to your accountant or the accounts department. To be properly in control *you* need to keep informed on financial aspects of the business.

167 Enforce the company's credit-control policy firmly. A sale isn't complete until the money is in the bank. Chase outstanding debts vigorously and don't be intimidated by large companies that want to delay payment. Their money should be earning interest for you.

168 Discuss management accounts with non-management staff to keep them involved and alert them to the need to control expenditure carefully.

169 Control the timing of your payments and do not pay sooner than necessary. Take advantage of early payment discounts only if they are genuinely beneficial.

Check suppliers' invoices carefully. Invest cash on hand wisely. Explain to your team how careful budgetary control improves cash flow.

170 Prevent abuse of expenses by showing people that you check their claims. Ask for details and insist on receipts. Check mileages.

Don't sign expenses automatically – the auditor might be the first to notice that someone you trust is double claiming. Make expenses rules clear to prevent any misunderstandings.

You might have been told that managers should be trusting. Sadly that trust would often be misplaced. In some recent research that compared honesty levels in handling money in different professions, even church ministers scored only 58 per cent. Members of the general public scored highest at 88 per cent. Don't be naïve: check.

171 If you are responsible for pricing don't be over-cautious; identify your place in the market and aim to give value for money. Successful companies are rarely the cheapest in their field.

172 Avoid giving discounts. Justify the price rather than give away profit. If your market is discount-oriented, anticipate with prices that are profitable after reductions.

If you're forced to make concessions, trade them off – ask for something in return: money 'up front' or staged payments.

Performance standards

People are often described as a company's most valuable resource, but some organizations, even with tight financial controls and a strong emphasis on quality, make little attempt to measure the individual contributions of their managers and staff – who are very expensive and, like other resources, must give value for money. Systematically monitor the performance of each member of your team.

173 Insist on high standards – reject anything less. Have a zero-defect policy along the lines of 'We provide only perfect products and a perfect after-sales service'. Of course your staff are fallible, but if you ask for 95 per cent reliability that's all you'll get. Your company can't survive with a failure rate of 5, or even 1 per cent.

Airline pilots must never crash; nurses must never drop babies!

174 Encourage staff to use initiative. Explain that problem solving and reacting well in a crisis are qualities deserving promotion but don't be annoyed if people make mistakes. Talk the situation through calmly and help them learn.

175 Measure and analyse absenteeism and staff turnover. Annual staff turnover percentage is calculated as the number of people who leave in the year divided by the average staff strength for the year multiplied by 100.

If 25 people leave your company in one year and average staff strength is 200, then staff turnover is $(25/200) \times 100 = 12.5$ per cent.

If staff turnover is above 10 per cent or absenteeism above 3 per cent (excluding holidays), don't blame external events. Look for causes within the organization, and look at the way you are managing. If you have a 5 per cent absentee rate and you need 20 people in your section you must employ 21 to be certain 20 will turn up. You could still be understaffed on Mondays and Fridays. Good managers have lower staff turnover and absenteeism in their sections, despite bad weather or unreliable public transport or even outbreaks of flu. If absenteeism/turnover is especially high in certain jobs, consider ways of making them more challenging and interesting.

176 Don't make people feel mistrusted. Show genuine interest in their work and ask questions. Don't spy on people or surprise them. Your trust will be returned by the majority of your team, but don't be deceived.

It is not unfair to drop in on staff at home who are absent ill, or to telephone to find out how they are progressing.

177 Become sensitive to 'atmosphere' as you walk the job. If your people are unhappy you need to know. Be alert for signs of ill-feeling between staff members.

178 If your organization has no performance appraisal system, go to your manager and explain that you want to discuss your progress in detail. Don't be brushed aside – explain that it is important to you and suggest that you meet to:

1. Review the content of the job, update your job description and consider any changes of emphasis.
2. Discuss in detail your actual performance for the last six months against your objectives.
3. Analyse your competence in each of the managerial skills (you could simply list the chapter headings of this book).
4. Agree measurable performance objectives for yourself for the coming half-year.
5. Draw up a training plan to add any knowledge and skills you may need to enhance your strengths, to correct any weaknesses and to develop your potential.

On pp. 62–63 you will find a management performance review form used by hundreds of companies. You will need to enlarge it to A4 size for your own use. Complicated appraisal forms can be confusing: the strength of this lies in its simplicity. School-report-type formats, in which appraisers award marks out of ten or tick boxes, are of little value. Section 3 of this form is far more searching. Don't be surprised if your manager needs persuading. His/her excuses might include:

'I'm too busy'; 'But I see you most days'; 'We don't need a form'; 'We've managed without it' and 'I'll always let you know if I'm not happy about something'.

None of these objectives is valid. Emphasize that you would like a full appraisal of your performance and that day-to-day conversations are not enough. After all, stock and finance are recorded daily but are still subject to more detailed checks at regular intervals.

The real reason for your manager's reluctance is probably nervousness, so give reassurance and, if it is new to both of you, learn together. Perhaps the first review will feel a little awkward but after that you will both wonder how you managed without it.

179 Create a performance review form for each functional role, substituting a different Section 3 into the management version, as shown on p. 68.

180 Bring your team together and hand out copies of the appropriate forms – and explain the purpose of systematically reviewing performance and its benefits. Explain that you will be pencilling in an identical form to prepare for the interview and that it will be inked in only after discussion at the meeting.

Impress upon people that, to be useful, the appraisal must be an honest exchange of views which might question the way you manage. Tell people they will see *everything* written on the form.

Make firm appointments for the interviews; ensure absolute privacy and allow no interruptions.

Relieve tension by welcoming the person, perhaps fetch a coffee, repeat the need for honesty during the five-point agenda and emphasize that the meeting is an 'inter-view' – a mutual opportunity to see. 'We're members of the same team. Our performance depends on each other.'

1   Review job content

Discuss the job functions. Have the document in front of you and, if there are any changes in the job, including any shift of emphasis, update the description. Have the new version typed up and issued.

Management Performance Review

A company will succeed only if managers (at all levels) are managing effectively.

This performance review (appraisal) form is designed to be used as the basis for a regular systematic review of managerial performance. Day-to-day contact with one's senior manager, though important, is not enough; a detailed discussion at length annually or ideally half-yearly is essential.

Method

The following method is recommended:

1. Briefing.
2. Preparation by the manager and the senior manager independently, using a copy of the form.
3. The interview in private without interruptions.
4. Completed review form seen by the appraiser's manager.
5. Follow-up. Implementation and monitoring of the plan.

Section 1.   Review of Job description

Discuss any changes of responsibility or shift of emphasis in your job and change the job description accordingly.

Are there any aspects of your job that you do not fully understand?

Section 2.   Performance Review

Discuss your performance since the last review.

Objectives agreed at last review	Actual performance

Comments:

Were there any obstacles outside your own control which prevented you from performing effectively?

Section 3.   Consider the Manager's Mastery of Essential Skills

(Discuss whether he/she ...)

Organizing ability	... deploys staff, money, materials and time wisely ... meets deadlines ... reviews and updates systems ... delegates whenever possible ... copes with emergencies ... ensures continuity when absent
Controlling	... supervises without stifling ... ensures regular feedback of important information ... keeps adequate records ... is in regular contact with all immediate subordinates ... spots 'early warning signals'
Leadership	... sets a good example ... inspires confidence and loyalty ... insists on high standards ... gets the team working harmoniously with a common purpose ...is consistent/fair ... agrees targets ... keeps staff informed ... retains staff
Planning	... makes realistic long-term plans ... establishes realistic targets ... plans well in short term ... keeps a diary ... establishes priorities
Staff selection	... prepares detailed job descriptions and person profiles ... screens effectively ... interviews skilfully ... judges objectively on facts ... avoids 'overselling' the job ... uses selection tests when appropriate ... always obtains references
Evaluating performance	... makes rational judgements ... identifies people's strengths/weaknesses/difficulties/potential and takes necessary action ... conducts regular performance review meetings with all subordinates
Training/developing the team	... has an up-to-date company/divisional/department training plan ... gears training to match objectives ... uses appropriate training methods ... records/evaluates training ... provides follow-up training
Decision making	... avoids making 'snap' decisions ... gathers all relevant information ... consults as appropriate ... anticipates problems ... advises all concerned
Communicating ability	... expresses him/herself clearly ... writes concise letters/memos ... listens ... uses the telephone well ... runs effective meetings

Comments

_____

_____

_____

_____

_____

_____

_____

_____

_____

Section 4.   Agree objectives for Next Half-Year

Objectives must be measurable and challenging.

Objective	Deadline
1.	
2.	
3.	
4.	
5.	
6.	

Section 5.   Training and Development Plan

The following development programme has been agreed. You are to make appropriate arrangements.

Training objective	The plan	Agreed deadline
1.		
2.		
3.		
4.		
5.		
6.		
7.		

Summary by 'appraiser'

Signed..............................

Comments by 'appraisee'

Signed..............................

Comments by 'appraiser's' manager

Signed..............................

Completed review form seen by 'appraisee'

Signed..............................

Date of next review................................

Section 3.   Consider Work Performance in Detail

(Discuss whether the salesperson . . .)

Planning	. . . devises realistic long-term plans . . . and accurate sales forecasts . . . has a one-year development plan for all major accounts . . . manages time effectively . . . sets an aim for every contact
Prospecting	. . . systematically scours the media and other sources for potential clients . . . uses the telephone professionally to qualify decision makers and makes appointments . . . establishes contact at a senior level . . . cultivates further contacts within client companies . . . obtains referrals from clients including parent/associate companies . . . builds network of contacts
Identifying and satisfying needs	. . . creates a favourable first impression . . . controls interviews subtly . . . asks questions and listens 'consultatively' . . . presents products enthusiastically and skilfully . . . explains relevant advantages and benefits
Dealing with sales resistance	. . . nullifies initial sales resistance . . . has developed successful techniques to deal with 'standard' objections . . . isolates 'specific' objections . . . and responds skilfully . . . keeps his/her knowledge of competition and of the market up to date . . . and uses it judiciously
Closing/account management	. . . asks for the order . . . again and again if necessary . . . negotiates firmly . . . resists giving discount . . . achieves a high proposal:order conversion rate . . . retains and develops clients . . . is prepared to do that little extra to help clients . . . follows up after the sale . . . checks on clients' continued satisfaction . . . remains in contact even when there is no immediate prospect of business
Administration	. . . keeps detailed up-to-date records . . . submits accurate reports on time . . . deals with matters promptly . . . meets deadlines . . . responds to correspondence within one working day . . . checks proposals, letters etc. carefully before signing
Other competencies	. . .communicates clearly, confidently and enthusiastically . . . maintains a high work rate . . . learns from experience . . . builds good relationships throughout our own organization . . . drives skilfully and safely

2 Discuss actual performance versus objectives

With measurable objectives there's no contention over achievement – you both know if the person has reached the agreed target. Find genuine reasons for poor performance and help the person learn from his/her mistakes.

3 Discuss each component of the job

Discuss the key skills required in the job, often referred to as 'competencies', and how the person matches them. Use questions beginning with 'what', 'when', 'how', 'who', 'which' and 'why' to encourage the interviewee to talk about his/her successes, mistakes, strengths, weaknesses and difficulties, and 'closed' questions, inviting a yes/no answer to clarify and confirm agreement.

Listen very closely to what the person says. To elicit more information use supplementary and reflective questions, 'Tell me more about that', 'So you're not happy about your security duties?' Use silences to draw out more information, and try to do no more than 40 per cent of the talking.

Give credit for good performance, and then the person will accept criticism. Always support your opinions with actual examples. There should be no surprises: problems and mistakes should have been discussed immediately – not stored up for the appraisal.

Don't work slavishly through each item in Section 3 in the printed sequence – make the form serve you. In particular try to avoid discussing problem after problem. Establish agreement and commitment and let the person see what you are writing.

4 Agree new objectives

As you reach agreement on objectives at any point in the interview, write them in this section. Remember, objectives must be specific. Get commitment to quality, quantity and cost targets and firm deadlines.

Make objectives realistic. You might need to moderate an

optimist's view or encourage a less confident person to be more ambitious.

5   Agree a training plan

Put together a schedule to satisfy the training needs discussed in the meeting. Training objectives should state specifically the required outcome. Don't automatically consider external training – most of the learning will be done in-company, but it must be properly planned.

Short courses, in-house or external, might be helpful in adding to or developing knowledge and skills. Prepare people for bigger jobs with personal coaching by delegating more work, by visits to clients and suppliers, or job rotation, but don't promise promotion.

Ensure that people accept responsibility for their own development and don't expect you to control their progress. When appropriate, encourage them to take evening classes or other training leading to professional qualifications.

Closing the interview

At the end of the interview run through the completed form and ask the interviewee to summarize. End the appraisal on a high note – the person must return to work feeling enthusiastic and confident.

Don't limit time for appraisals. The interview finishes when you achieve its aims. Appraisals for senior people are likely to be lengthy because their responsibilities and duties are wide, but interviewing a junior team member who needs counselling can take as long.

Do not discuss remuneration at performance reviews. People will be reluctant to admit to difficulties if they believe it will affect their earnings.

If your policy is to review people's salaries on each anniversary of their appointment, you can avoid the problem by appraising everyone three months after they join the company, or take up a position, then half-yearly. With this system the annual salary review falls between appraisals and you spread the workload evenly throughout the year. Systematic performance appraisal doesn't mean filling in forms twice a year – it's a meeting of minds to boost the performance of each member of your team. Their combined performance represents your performance.

181 Encourage staff to monitor their own performance.

182 Have frequent interim meetings to discuss progress against objectives.

183 When things go wrong, be more interested in discovering the causes and solving the problem than in blaming people.

184 Don't make your staff afraid to admit problems. A reputation for losing your temper will make people conceal mistakes until those mistakes become full-scale crises. Encourage people to come to you with answers.

185 Use a skills review and training planner (see p. 72) to give you an up-to-date overview of the team's abilities. You will have adequate cover during holiday periods and be able to plan ahead for the loss of valuable experience when key people retire.

Material resources

Poor control costs money. Inefficiency and waste have to be financed by your customers, and that can lose you business.

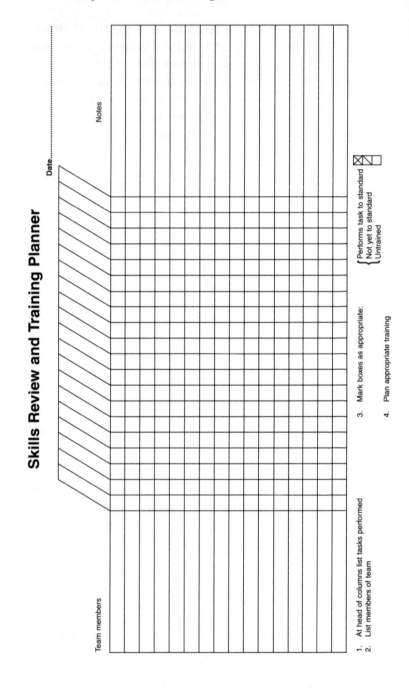

Skills Review and Training Planner

Date.......

Team members

Notes

1. At head of columns list tasks performed
2. List members of team

3. Mark boxes as appropriate:
   - Performs task to standard
   - Not yet to standard
   - Untrained

4. Plan appropriate training

186 Operate strict quality controls. Professional and government buyers insist on national quality standards, so stay competitive. Persuade senior management to operate controls in your organization.

Customers in all markets are becoming more discerning. Quality control in McDonalds restaurants is very strict and the same standards apply worldwide. Cooks must turn, never flip, burgers; french fries must be thrown away if they are unsold seven minutes after they're cooked; sales staff must make eye contact and smile at every customer.

Train your people to achieve similar standards from the very beginning: don't settle for anything less. And enforce those standards strictly day to day. Make people responsible for their own quality checks – standards drop if people expect others to correct their mistakes. Invite customers to comment on service and pass their reports to senior management.

187 Pay close attention to stock control and stock rotation. Poor management encourages abuse and this can be very costly.

188 Monitor all stock and equipment carefully. Tight security will discourage dishonesty. Be strict with defaulters – dismissal and legal proceedings should be the rule, but you must be sure of what has happened. If equipment is disappearing, bring in the police or a professional security organization.

189 Make it clear that nothing is to be taken home without your permission. Introduce a simple system and then be generous. Make sure that everyone understands that taking anything without permission is theft and will always result at least in dismissal and almost certainly prosecution.

190 Train anyone responsible for receiving deliveries to check things carefully and to sign only after they have counted every item.

191 Liaise closely with suppliers, especially if you work for a manufacturing company. Streamline your operation with a JIT (just in time) system so that items arrive when they are actually needed. Components delivered to Nissan factories in the morning are assembled that day and are ready for sale as part of a complete vehicle the same evening. Storage space is kept to a minimum and capital is better invested elsewhere.

192 Ensure tight security at all points of entry to your premises and train your staff to be alert at all times. Receptionists must not allow anyone to pass unvetted. In some buildings anyone wearing a uniform or a white coat can stroll in unchallenged – and remove equipment.

193 Enforce health and safety rules. You are liable for accidents in your section and you could be fined or go to prison through negligence.

Serious accidents happen not only with machine tools and on building sites. Trailing leads, a broken electric socket or loose floor tiles are all potential killers. Written notices or entries in the staff handbook are not enough: train your staff always to be careful. Be firm with people who break the rules. Do not allow skylarking. People die at work every year because of jokes that go wrong.

Information you need

A department is part of a company-wide network. Your

company is part of an industry. Your industry connects with other industries as part of the country's economy. You may even need to take an international view because most markets are now global.

You must have effective channels of information to keep your knowledge up to date.

194 Gather enough accurate information to enable you to monitor progress and update the plan. Use your trade association and other external bodies for information on market trends or competitor activity. Calculate your market share and that of your main competitors. Compile a dossier on each competitor, add every snippet of information, and keep it up to date. What can you learn from them? Pass information on quickly to people who need it.

195 Insist on prompt control information from staff. You need to know immediately if there is a risk of losing a customer. Relationships that have taken years to develop can be shattered in minutes. Customer care is everyone's responsibility, but especially yours.

196 Don't ask for information that you don't really need: it's a waste of time that could be used more productively.

197 Conduct regular briefing meetings not only to bring your team up to date but to gather information.

198 Make someone responsible for the section noticeboard: to keep it up to date and tidy. If you publish a house journal or newsletter, make sure people look forward to receiving it and actually read it. Perhaps send it to customers. But never expect written material to have the same impact as good face-to-face communication.

199 Explain to people who have access to confidential information that breaches of confidence will make them liable to summary dismissal, and include this in their contract of employment.

In successful businesses there are very few secrets but some matters are bound to be confidential and people in positions of trust must be totally reliable.

200 Keep paperwork under control and filing/records up to date.

201 Read correspondence and reports carefully before signing them. If you discover a mistake later, it is entirely your fault.

202 When appropriate, confirm agreed action in writing, especially when dealing with people you know are unreliable.

203 Use 'benchmarking' and key ratios to measure the effectiveness of your operation, for example,

- sales per employee
- profit per employee
- service costs per customer
- customers per engineer.

Don't base judgements on instinct. If you can't measure it you can't manage it. In your attempt to improve performance change only one variable at a time; otherwise you will not know what is causing the improvement.

204 Show control information on graphs and charts – patterns are easier to see. Use moving annual graphs to plot trends and to avoid erratic, meaningless ups and downs.

You can't manage effectively unless you are in control. You can't know everything – but be sure that you receive the information you need in time to enable you to take prompt decisive action.

Personal Action Plan

Control

Action	Target date	Achieved

6

How to train and develop

Successful managers systematically train their people at all levels, not only because they care about them but because it is profitable. The evidence is overwhelming: trained managers and staff outperform their untrained competitors.

Practice on its own is not enough. If someone is doing something incorrectly and they practise hard enough, eventually they will learn to do it wrong perfectly.

Think of training as accelerated experience. It enables your staff to learn from the successes and mistakes of others and to avoid the pain and cost of learning the hard way. The learner moves through four stages:

- Unconscious incompetence – not being able to do something or not even being aware of their ignorance.
- Conscious incompetence – becoming aware.
- Conscious competence – learning how to do something but having to concentrate hard on each stage of the process.

- Unconscious competence – being able to carry out the task effortlessly.

205 Create a training plan to support the trading plan. You need people in the right place at the right time, equipped with the right knowledge and skills to make the plan a reality.

206 Systematically develop each member of your team. Those with most potential will be the first to leave if you don't. Victor Rice, President of Varity Corporation (previously Massey Ferguson) of Canada said: 'We have a succession planning process that says: "if the guy in this job gets run over by a bus tomorrow who would you put in there?" If you have enough time to select the person you think will be right with more training – perhaps a two-year horizon – who is it? And if you have a five-year horizon is it a different person?'

207 Help people to learn jobs other than their own to broaden experience, provide cover in emergencies, avoid boring repetitive work, and improve efficiency.

Induction and initial training

Newcomers feel lonely, nervous and uneasy because initially they are unable to make a useful contribution: plan suitable training to introduce them to the company, your department and to the job.

208 Arrange for new people to arrive after the usual start time on their first day. Welcome them personally.

209 Use the job description as a basis for initial training. Consider what knowledge and skills are necessary, how they can be acquired, and in what order.

210 Nominate a sponsor – a colleague to whom the newcomer can turn for help. This will ideally be someone of similar age and interests, someone to whom they will relate. This is not a training responsibility; the colleague acts more as a 'buddy'.

211 If you use experienced staff to teach new recruits, train them to train. They must not pass on bad habits.

German engineering companies have for many years trained experienced engineers to train others. They are then promoted to the position of 'Meister'. This system has probably made a significant contribution to Germany's reputation for high-quality engineering.

212 Remember to train people transferred within the company. They will not need company induction, but they need an introduction to your department and to the job.

People who join you from another company to do a similar job need to be trained to do things your way, and 'unlearning' can be difficult. Many companies have a policy of not recruiting from competitors, preferring to develop their own people.

Listen for people to say 'we', meaning *your* organization, not the one they have recently left. It's an important milestone and it means the person now considers himself/herself to be one of your team.

How people learn

Sitting beside an expert will not turn someone into a competent performer, any more than a concert-goer can learn to play a musical instrument by watching a virtuoso.

213 People learn through their senses, especially by seeing and doing, so don't just tell: show and coach.

214 Put learners at ease, because if they are tense they cannot learn. If people don't understand, encourage them to ask questions without feeling guilty or foolish.

215 Don't rush training because you are busy. The pace must be determined by the person's ability to learn, not how quickly you can speak. Give people time to consolidate and apply what they have learnt before moving on to the next stage.

216 Always give people a reason for learning. Tell them how they are going to benefit: 'This new procedure will save you at least an hour a day, Jim, so...'

217 Skill and knowledge can be taught but attitudes are only learnt by example. They are contagious. Your staff will be enthusiastic, loyal, helpful, punctual and conscientious only if you set an example.

Consider what attitudes are important in your team, that is, how would you like your customers, internal and external, to describe your team? The top ten answers from Invicta delegates are: honest, enthusiastic, helpful, loyal, knowledgeable, conscientious, polite, efficient, cooperative and trustworthy.

There are important recruitment implications here. Do not recruit a dishonest, rude, lazy person and expect training to change them! Personality and attitudes change only very slowly.

Identifying training needs

Consider how training can improve everyone's performance and how you will try to fill positions in the future by promoting from within rather than relying on competitors to train for you.

218 Train to keep ahead of the competition. IBM expect their staff to receive ten days off-the-job training every year.

As your business moves forward, new products, systems, policies and markets generate the need for training. Training is unending. Progress is impossible without it and in the future, as the rate of change accelerates, so the need for training will increase.

219 Review everyone's performance from the top and train to consolidate strengths, correct weaknesses and develop potential. Help people recognize training as an exciting opportunity, not as unpleasant treatment or a form of corrective punishment.

220 Invite customers to comment on your standard of service and to suggest ways that it could be improved. Train all staff who come into contact with customers, face to face, by telephone or in writing, to communicate professionally.

221 Provide training to keep all staff informed about your products, systems, policies and the competition. Even when the knowledge is not essential to people's work, it will help them feel involved.

Planning training

Like all business activities, training must be directed at achieving clearly defined objectives. If it is aimless it will achieve nothing.

Some motivation training focuses on the importance of a positive mental attitude – 'think win'. This is important but it must never be seen as a substitute for skill. A boxer, however confident, will lose if he doesn't know how to defend himself.

222 Select the most appropriate training methods: coaching, off-the-job, individual or group instruction, distance learning, an external course, guided reading or a combination of all methods.

223 Never conduct skills training without preparation. Expect to spend much longer planning the training than conducting it. Remind yourself of the learner's lack of, or limited, experience and consider how long it took you to become competent at the job involved.

Carefully analyse tasks: identify (i) stages – the sequence of events and (ii) key points – hints that will make sure each stage is carried out properly.

Help the learner move smoothly from the known to the unknown with EDIP – Explanation, Demonstration, Imitation, Practice. Relax coaching only when you are satisfied that the person is competent.

224 Cover complex subjects, especially technical training, in a series of linked training sessions with time between them for people to practise what they have learnt. Give continuing support and encouragement to maintain momentum and reinforce the learning.

225 Distinguish between knowledge (things the learner needs to know) and skills (things they need to be able to do). Make each training module a complete entity.

Use an introduction that captures people's interest by giving them a reason for learning, and cover the material in a logical sequence.

Summarize to reiterate the main points and test the learner to make sure you have achieved your objectives. Test both understanding (the rationale) and retention.

226 Make time during working hours for training. Short, regular sessions work best, causing minimal interruption to the smooth running of the business and maintaining people's interest. Whenever possible, hold sessions early in the day.

227 Most of the knowledge and skills your team need are within your company, but when necessary bring in specialists to conduct training. Manufacturers and suppliers will often provide training for no charge.

228 On-the-job coaching from you is the most important training – in the office, in the warehouse, on the sales floor or out in the field. It also underlines your role as the team leader and demonstrates the high standards you expect.

Move from a slow step-by-step approach with newcomers to a fine-tuning technique as they gain experience.

Keep your own knowledge and skill up to date by seeking people with greater knowledge to train you.

Training individuals

Each member of your team has different training and development needs. Some may be having difficulty with their present jobs, others need new knowledge and skills to cope with extra responsibilities, and some you are grooming for promotion.

229 Pace training to suit the learner's speed, which depends not only on their level of intelligence but also their age. Learning is a skill, and something people are better at immediately after leaving full-time education than 20 years later when they are probably out of practice.

230 Interactive video programmes or teach-yourself manuals help people to progress at their own pace and quickly pay for themselves. However, solitary trainees can easily become demotivated, so stay in close contact.

231 When you ask other managers to train your people, explain precisely what you want, to prevent their being used merely as part of the other manager's operation.

Training groups

Sometimes it will be sensible to train your staff in groups.

232 When a number of people have a similar training need it is more efficient to bring them together for training – they will benefit from learning together. Limit groups to a maximum of twelve. Use a range of training methods: discussion, syndicate work, case studies, management games and role playing. Robert Burns wrote 200 years ago:

> O wad some Pow'r the giftie gie us
> To see oursels as others see us!

Video recordings enable staff to watch themselves in action. If you don't have the authority to decide, persuade your manager to buy a good video camera to add a new dimension to your training sessions. If this fails, buy one with your own money and demonstrate its effectiveness. You could rent it to other managers!

233 Hold the training in quiet, well-ventilated, comfortable surroundings. A low temperature is better than too much warmth, and don't allow smoking. Arrange seating so that everyone can hear and see. A U-shaped configuration is ideal.

234 Talk to everyone and keep them all involved. Be especially careful not to overlook people sitting close to you. Ask questions to keep people's attention, float questions to the entire group, give them time to consider and then nominate the person to answer: Pose, Pause, Pounce. Socrates' technique of asking questions that helped people work things out for themselves is far more effective than giving the answers.

235 Use visual aids: products, overhead projector slides, videos, flipcharts, 35-mm slides, and so on: visual information is more readily understood and remembered longer.

236 Provide plenty of handouts rather than expecting people to write everything down. Unless they know shorthand they won't keep up.

It will help the team if you invite them to write down the most important points. You can probably remember taking an exam and trying to recall information. You are more likely to have retrieved it if you took the information in through the eyes rather than through the ears. You search for a visual image, not a sound.

237 Avoid distracting mannerisms and catch-phrases. Ask a colleague to tell you if you have any (or, better still, use that video camera to record yourself training), and then concentrate on removing them.

238 If a training session lasts for more than an hour, give the group a short break. Tell people precisely when you want them back: 'Back at 10.20, please', not 'Let's have a five-minute break'.

239 Keep the pace moving along but don't speak too quickly or try to include too much.

Incorporate as much practical work as possible. A 'doing' exercise at least every 20 minutes keeps everyone involved.

240 Ask members of the team or other managers to conduct training sessions, but always brief them carefully on the objective. Ask them how they propose to cover the subject: you must be satisfied that the training will match the high standard you and your team expect. Other managers will be flattered and you will demonstrate to your team the importance of good interdepartmental relations.

Developing potential

It is your duty to help each member of your team to achieve their full potential.

241 Use projects and assignments to develop analytical and leadership skills and to identify and test team members who are suitable for promotion.

Explain what is required and then ask the person to summarize to confirm their understanding. To help less experienced staff, invite them to come back to you with their project and check their progress: 'How do you intend to ...?' 'What about ...?', 'What will you do if ...?'

242 Use job rotation to accelerate the experience of high-flyers. People destined for the top need experience in as many areas of the organization as possible.

Japanese companies develop general managers, not specialists; follow their example. Promotion age to first-line management in Japan is 33 – in the West it is 27. People must be in a variety of positions long enough to prove their ability and see the effect of their own decisions. This will probably not take less than 12 to 18 months.

In flat organization structures most job changes will be horizontal. Consider ways of increasing people's breadth of responsibility.

243 Encourage ambitious people to take the initiative by studying for professional qualifications, reading, taking evening classes or distance learning programmes, including Open University courses. If you agree that a course is relevant, at least offer to contribute to the cost.

244 If your company does not have a resource centre, suggest starting one. It will soon become a valuable asset for people who are career-minded.

Limitations of training

Although it is difficult to imagine a person at work being overtrained, there is a point at which more training does not achieve a commensurate return.

245 Do not expect training to perform miracles. If you have put an unsuitable person into a job, increasing the training effort is not the answer – you are simply increasing the cost of your mistake and delaying the inevitable. You must remove the person immediately.

246 Train to graft on knowledge and skills, not to indoctrinate or brainwash people. Your aim should be to benefit the company by helping each member of your team achieve their potential.

But if you can help your staff become more self-confident and assertive, less shy and dependent, then why not? Such changes happen very slowly as a result of helping people to believe in themselves, and can help to correct harmful early conditioning.

Watch confidence increase as competence grows, but it takes time.

Evaluating training

Training is never free. Even on-the-job coaching costs the time of the trainer and the trained. Thus its pay-off needs to be measured.

247 Evaluate the effectiveness of training: whether it achieved what you intended, and if not, why not. Insist on value from your training budget as with any other expenditure. Brief people carefully before they undergo any training, whether internal or external. Agree objectives and ask them to compile an action plan during the training. Debrief them on their return and monitor with them their progress against their plan.

Train your people hard – as they succeed, so will you. Managing a team in business is very similar to running a sports team. Success cannot be achieved without very careful attention to training.

Personal Action Plan

Training and development

Action	Target date	Achieved

7

How to solve people problems

People problems must be identified and solved as quickly as possible. Small problems grow to medium-sized problems which grow into full-scale crises if they are ignored. Problems don't go away.

If necessary, seek advice, but you must act or you might be swamped by something you thought was trivial. It's easy to be a manager when things are going well but the real test is how you respond when there is a problem.

248 Watch out for early warning signals. 'Walking the job' is the best way to stay involved. You'll detect even small problems.

249 Don't dwell on problems. Worrying achieves nothing and you'll become depressed. Concentrate on finding solutions.

250 If you can't handle a problem ask your manager for advice. Don't try to muddle through – things will inevitably get worse.

251 Do what's right, not what's easy or popular in awkward situations.

252 Don't pass the buck. People problems in your department are your problems – don't send staff to the human resources department.

253 Set a good example by always being loyal to the company. When there are difficulties don't criticize the company or senior management.

254 Provide an opportunity for people to raise problems at work. Use departmental meetings where people will feel more secure with their colleagues around them, then concentrate the group's attention on finding answers.

255 Represent your team with pride when dealing with senior management. If they are right to complain about working conditions or pay, tell your manager and state their case fully.

256 Solve problems by talking to people. A skilfully conducted interview will tell you what's wrong and point the way to a solution.

Don't use interviews to assert your authority except over serious disciplinary problems. If you encourage your people to speak freely you'll learn what you need to know – and gain their confidence.

257 Listen. If you've listened for three-quarters of an interview it hasn't been out of your control – it's been a success. If you do most of the talking all you'll hear is what you know already.

Use open questions: usually 'what', 'where', 'when', 'how' or 'which'? Listen and adapt to the personality of the interviewee. Reserved people need time and encouragement to answer fully. Contain very talkative people by summarizing and, where appropriate, asking closed questions to elicit yes/no answers.

Use supplementary questions or probes to draw out further details, and reflective questions to encourage people to enlarge on what they have just said – 'Oh?', 'Really?', 'Is that important to you?'

258 Always conduct interviews in private. Make sure you can't be overheard. If you work in an open-plan office you might even have to leave the building.

259 Never prejudge. To prejudge is to be prejudiced. What you think is a disciplinary matter could be a domestic problem, and the individual might need counselling.

Unsatisfactory performance

To most managers, the word 'discipline' suggests punishment. To you, it should mean helping poor performers to improve.

260 The time the person needs to reach an acceptable standard of performance will depend on the nature of the job, their previous experience and the quality of training they are receiving. If someone is making very slow progress you must interview them to investigate the shortfall.

261 Explain to the person that their performance is unsatisfactory. Someone used to a less testing atmosphere might have difficulty in reaching your standards. If they don't understand what's needed, talk through their progress using facts to help them appreciate the problem.

262 Check that your standards are realistic. If few in your team are achieving them, you could be expecting too much.

263 Be totally honest and explain your dissatisfaction clearly.

264 Give specific examples of unacceptable behaviour: 'Your expenses during the sales convention between 17 and 24 July were £67 above the agreed limit', not 'These business trips seem to be getting a bit expensive'.

265 Don't make accusations you can't substantiate: you could be presented with a private summons. Be sure of your facts.

266 Show disappointment, not anger. Staying calm is far more effective than losing your temper. If you are angry, keep it under control – don't say or do anything you might regret later.

267 Disciplinary interviewing doesn't mean punishment. Your aims are (i) to discover the reasons for the person's unsatisfactory performance or behaviour, and (ii) to agree a plan that will help them improve.

268 Plan the interview in advance. Anticipate problems that could occur and decide how you will deal with them.

269 Ask for reasons for poor performance. Remember that it is often more difficult for older people to acquire knowledge and learn new skills. They'll take longer to move up the performance ladder, so give them time to adjust.

270 Decide whether poor performance is because of lack of effort, motivation or training – or a combination of all three. Agree a plan to improve the person's performance. Help them by setting measurable targets, seek a commitment to improve, and set a deadline.

271 Remember that talented people sometimes become a problem because they are not being stretched. More responsibility or tougher targets could be the answer.

272 Be firm. Your staff will be pleased to have a strong manager. If you are weak, others will take advantage and your high achievers will lose interest.

273 Be fair and consistent. Your team want a strong manager but not a bully. Prepare carefully for disciplinary interviews. Use job descriptions and performance records, study facts, follow company procedure – then you can help a person become more effective.

274 Follow company policy on oral and written warnings. If your firm is unionized, keep to the agreed procedure for discipline.

275 If you are faced with a very difficult interview don't take the easy way out by asking someone else to conduct it. A role play, with a colleague or your manager playing the interviewee, will help you.

276 Keep yourself up to date on your company's disciplinary policy. If a problem flares up you need to know what authority you have and at what stage you should involve your manager.

Do you have the authority to dismiss summarily or suspend on full pay? If you don't, find out immediately.

277 Remember that employment law is liable to rapid change. Precedents are set from day to day in tribunals which make conventional books on the subject unreliable. Consider subscribing to an update service such as Croner's in the UK or telephone the Advisory, Conciliation and Arbitration Service (ACAS) for immediate advice.

278 If someone finds a job difficult don't blame them. You, your company, possibly your customers are all suffering but it's the person who is failing at their job who is most unhappy. It's up to you to rescue that person – if the work is beyond them, is redeployment possible? If not, you must counsel them. It will be better for them to seek employment elsewhere than to battle on. They will become stressed and unwell, particularly when you have to issue disciplinary warnings.

279 Don't create an unnecessary job to avoid dismissing someone. If encouragement and training don't work you must move on to the next stage of the disciplinary procedure.

280 If you have inherited someone whose performance is unsatisfactory, agree targets and train them hard to bring them up to standard. If that fails, you must persist, but be prepared to instigate disciplinary procedures.

Explain that standards are minimum acceptable levels of performance. Employment law is not intended to make life difficult for you. If you are fair and reasonable you have nothing to fear, but when in doubt, check.

281 If someone seems out of their depth don't plan immediately how you can get rid of them – that's constructive dismissal. But when you're sure that someone is unsuitable for the job they must leave. Don't send them to another department – unless by some remarkable coincidence they have untapped skills which are needed there.

In the UK, at present, employees have legal protection against unfair or wrongful dismissal after 24 months with your organization, but you'll know well before that if they are unsuitable. You brought them in so you must remove them – gently, yes, but they have to go.

282 When a final warning proves unproductive the dismissal becomes inevitable. Keep the dismissal interview brief and to the point. However pleading, upset or tearful the person, you must not be dissuaded.

Attend to any necessary administration and arrange for the person to leave immediately to avoid unpleasantness or embarrassment.

Handling grievances

When someone in your team comes to you with a grievance, be prepared to talk it through. With skilful questions
and careful listening you might discover the beginnings of
a larger problem. Most grievances are the result of breakdowns in communication or perceived unfairness.

283 Familiarize yourself with the company's grievance procedure: it will be written into everyone's
contract of employment. The initial step is usually to
approach the immediate manager and, if that doesn't
resolve the matter, the person concerned then has the right
to an interview with a more senior person.

284 Keep in close contact with your staff, but don't
crowd them.

285 Have regular departmental meetings and
encourage people to air any grievances and
suggest realistic solutions. Don't allow people just to complain – they must be constructive.

286 Keep staff informed as much as possible. There
could be misunderstandings if people rely on
general gossip for information.

287 At grievance interviews let interviewees explain
their grievance fully. If you interrupt you won't
gather as much information. But concentrate on facts, not
emotional arguments. Grievance interviewing is 99 per cent
listening.
　　As the pace of life increases stress creates enormous
pressures both at work and in people's private lives. It is

estimated that 60 per cent of sickness absence is stress-related. If members of your team are worried they cannot give their full commitment to the job.

Be patient. If a person is angry they will calm down if you allow them time to talk. Any employee who comes to you must feel that their grievance is being taken seriously.

Use silence and eye contact to draw out information.

288 If appropriate, make notes and summarize the grievance to make sure that you have fully understood. The person might decide to reconsider before you take any action.

289 Never be blackmailed by people who threaten to leave because of pay or benefits. Make it clear that you won't make *anyone* a special case. If there is unfairness, review the situation for everyone involved, not only complainants.

290 If the grievance concerns difficult relationships, check the facts by speaking to other people. Don't make a decision based on one person's point of view.

291 Never rush your decision – but don't delay unreasonably. Gather together all the facts, make your decision, perhaps after consultation with your manager, and then sleep on it.

292 Give reasons for unpopular decisions. If you explain them by saying 'because it's company policy' or 'because I say so' you'll alienate your staff.

Communicate the outcome clearly and consider how you will keep everyone better informed in future.

Counselling

As a manager of integrity and good judgement you have a responsibility to give help and support even when the problem is not work-related.

293 Encourage the person to talk about their problem. Ask questions that will help work out the solution. Usually the conversation will simply reaffirm the answer they have already arrived at, but talking it though will be reassuring.

294 Don't advise on matters on which you are not expert. Imagine the consequences of giving wrong advice on marital, emotional, health or financial problems! Use questions to help the person decide to see a professional adviser.

295 Respect confidences. Talk to others only if you have permission.

296 Don't pry into private matters, but if someone's work is suffering you have a right to take action. If one of your team is often absent through ill-health, arrange for them to have a medical check-up to ensure that they are fit enough to do the job. If they are not, take advice on your options.

297 If you temporarily adjust someone's work standards, tell other members of the team. You may be under pressure to explain, but don't betray confidences.

298 Middle-aged people can become bored or dispirited if younger managers are overtaking them. It's reasonable for them to ask about their future. If you consider that they are unlikely to be promoted, help them achieve a balanced view. Promotion means bigger responsibilities and bigger problems. Is that what they really want?

Look for opportunities to increase the range of jobs; perhaps it is possible to provide more challenge without promotion.

Reassure, emphasize their value to the team, but never mislead people about their career prospects.

299 Be prepared to make the first move with personal problems. If you suspect one of your staff has a drink or drug problem, don't tackle it head on. Discuss performance and ask for reasons for the reduction in quality and quantity of their work, or their poor time-keeping and so on.

If health and safety regulations are in danger of being broken, or the person drives a company vehicle or operates potentially dangerous equipment, insist on a medical examination. You must then be guided by your company policy.

300 If one of your team has BO or bad breath it is unfair not to tackle the problem. Talk to the person in private. Be straightforward, but always be tactful. Say 'I'm sorry to have to talk to you about this, John, but I have noticed that sometimes you seem to have a problem with body odour. Do you know why that might be?' Ask for reasons. Don't assume that they are neglecting their personal hygiene – the person might be very tense or have a glandular condition. Bad breath could be caused by a dietary problem. Whatever the cause, work together to find a solution.

Don't be weak and avoid the problem. It is unkind to drop hints, leave sprays around or ask someone else to approach the person.

Dealing with problems can be difficult or embarrassing, but it's part of your job. When someone comes to you for help, never turn them away or tell them to 'pull themselves together' – if this is your reaction you will cause more unhappiness and prolong the impact of the problem. By responding sympathetically you will earn respect, resolve the difficulty more quickly and restore concentration to the achievement of the task in hand.

Personal Action Plan

People problems

Action	Target date	Achieved

it's always been done that way' aren't reasons to continue a bad system.

Successful companies don't accept that established ideas are right. Inventions are often the result of looking at problems in different ways.

307 If you are unhappy with a decision from senior management, discuss it calmly with your manager. If you are still unhappy you have three choices: to accept the decision and give it your full support, to take the matter to a higher authority through the grievance procedure, or to resign. Do not accept the decision grudgingly and criticize it in front of your team. You're not paid to cause dissent within the company or confuse staff, and you won't win loyalty by disowning unpopular decisions.

308 Worrying achieves nothing. Think things through and don't be reluctant to ask for help if you need it.

309 When one of your people asks for special treatment, think carefully before agreeing. You're not consistent if you give your secretary extended holidays but turn down other people's requests. They will feel aggrieved.

310 If you grant a one-off concession, make the situation clear. If you let people go home early on two consecutive Fridays because business is quiet, that does not give them the right to leave early the following week.

Consultation, involvement and empowerment

Years ago managers presided over their department. They made decisions which were carried out by their subordinates. There were bosses and workers. Henry Ford dismissed Lee Iococca for having the audacity to challenge a decision. Iococca went on to become CEO of Chrysler Corporation!

Today the situation is very different. Of course managers have to make some single-handed decisions, when the need for confidentiality or urgency dictates. But whenever possible decision making should be devolved.

The modern manager empowers the team and individuals to make most decisions. After all, they are on the spot and have more information. If they are trained and understand any constraints on them they can respond more quickly and appropriately to the customer's needs. Everyone benefits: *the team*, who are more involved and motivated; *the customer*, who gets a speedier more relevant response; *the manager*, who is able to get on with his/her job; and *the business*, which runs more efficiently.

Between these two extremes – unilateral decision making and empowerment – there lies a range of options, including consultation, where the manager decides after consulting the team, and joint decision making, when the manager has an equal say and no greater influence than other team members.

You need the full range of skills and must decide which option best matches your style and the needs of the situation.

311 Always listen to advice inside and outside work, especially from more experienced managers. In the bar or at parties, ask questions, be quiet and listen. Learn from people's experience.

312 Listen carefully to everyone's point of view. Don't assume that people are wrong because they are young or new to the company. They might see matters with a clarity you've lost.

When Fort Dunlop was taken over by Sumitomo, the Japanese management asked for money-saving ideas from the workforce. A junior employee saved the company £100 000 a year in electricity payments by suggesting that every other fluorescent light in the huge factory needn't be used, and he'd had the idea for years!

313 Make use of the special expertise of your staff and colleagues. Use people's experience in different markets and different countries to extend your options. Familiarize yourself with your own team roles and those of your colleagues. Draw on each other's strengths.

314 When you must make the decision, consult others and consider their ideas, but remember that your business isn't a democracy. A manager who decides on the basis of a show of hands has abdicated responsibility. Value your team's experience and tell them you want their views. Listen to them, but, as the manager, you have the final decision. Make it clear that if you decide not to accept their views it isn't because you haven't listened. If you want a high input from your team, surround yourself with people who want to be involved, not staff who prefer to be told what to do. Your team must reflect your style. People leave jobs if their manager's style doesn't satisfy their needs. New people need a more directive approach from you but you can return to your consultative style as they grow into the job. You must be adaptable. Staff rely on you to behave consistently, but in an emergency or when you are unable to reveal information you will need to tell, not ask: if the building is on fire you don't ask for everyone's view on the fire drill!

Managers who tend to make decisions democratically inspire least confidence. Even cooperatives are not democracies. They involve everyone in the decision-making process but it's the managers who have final responsibility.

The venue for a Christmas party or how to furnish a recreation room can be a majority decision but company policy cannot. The popular view isn't always right for the firm, particularly in difficult times. Everyone wants a strong manager, one they are proud to work for.

315 Never deceive when making decisions. Don't consult and then ignore people's views; never abuse joint decisions by vote rigging: people will never trust you again.

316 Talk to people who will be affected by your decision. People accept decisions through persuasive conversation, not through imposition.

Explain the rationale and listen carefully to any counter-arguments. Sell your decision strongly and modify it only if you are persuaded by new evidence. Be strong but not inflexible.

317 Lead by example in decision making. Demonstrate how to consult and sell decisions and allow your team to make decisions affecting their work.

318 Develop a style that works best for you. Your style is determined mainly by your personality but you do have a choice. If you are inclined to be dominant you can become more consultative; if you are more reserved you can develop a more thrusting approach and 'tell' when necessary. Work at the change over a period: an overnight swing will shock and confuse.

319 Don't try to cover everything in the procedures manual. Your people need freedom to make decisions but within reasonable constraints. You need job descriptions for good organization but not in such detail that they stifle initiative. Explain why prescribed methods must be followed, but people mustn't become an extension of the machinery.

320 Encourage decision making at the most junior level possible – but you are still accountable.
Empower people by giving them freedom to act. It is frustrating for them if they have to keep coming to you for permission.

321 As people prove capable, gradually increase their decision-making authority. Don't then snatch it back. Train them and be available to give advice when asked.

Timing

The right decision too late is no more use than the wrong decision early.

322 Don't make snap judgements of people or situations. Impressions based on appearance or quickly-formed opinion can be totally wrong, even damaging.

323 Don't make decisions hastily. Some companies like to be first with new products; others watch for their mistakes. Only do nothing intentionally, and don't get left behind. Gather information and watch competitors very closely: carry out company searches and put your name on their mailing lists.

If a rival is pulling ahead, find out what they are doing, then reduce their advantage. Talk to competitors. There's no need for animosity. Provided you learn more than you reveal and don't give away any secrets, why not talk to rivals?

324 Don't be influenced by fictional managers on television or in films who make decisions on the spot. Successful managers don't behave like that. Buying an oil company or firing a director is not a decision to make instantly – that's fantasy, not dynamic management. Important decisions take weeks or months of planning and consideration.

Making the decision

When 1000 people were asked to list the most important qualities they look for in their manager, 'decisiveness' appeared in more than 80 per cent of their lists.

325 When you have two alternatives, it helps to list points in favour and points against each choice. Grade points 1 to 10 according to how much they should influence the decision. For example, *For:* I will give Des responsibility for the launch of the new product to develop his experience (10). It will free me to consult the team on next year's budgets (7) and so on. *Against:* It's a major project and probably too soon for Des at this stage (8). The lead time is tight and would put Des under undue pressure (9) and so on.

Calculate the odds, know the facts and take risks if the company has a good chance of success.

All successful businesses take risks; there's no such thing as a certainty – some ventures generate profit, some are experiments for the future. Risk taking is like gambling. With the willpower not to spend beyond your limit, taking carefully calculated risks won't damage your career.

Acting on decisions

Making a decision is only the beginning. Often the greater challenge is to implement it.

326 Set realistic times for implementing decisions. Directors make strategic decisions which often take years to become reality. Junior managers make decisions with a short-term impact.

327 When you make decisions, communicate them clearly. Some good decision makers forget to tell staff exactly what is required so their decisions are ineffective.

328 Don't be surprised or annoyed if staff ask 'why?'. You should have told them. Explain decisions early and provide answers. It's natural for people to resist change, so help them accept decisions. Ease your team's fears by explaining the rationale and the expected outcome.

Improving your decision-making ability

As you win promotions you will have to make ever bigger decisions. No one makes the right decision every time, but if you improve your success rate from 80 to 90 per cent you will advance from competent to outstanding.

329 Read a book on creativity to develop your skill. A good one to start with is *Creative Thinking and Brainstorming* by J. Geoffrey Rawlinson.

330 Discuss with your manager participative decision-making techniques to secure everyone's input and commitment. Consider using project teams to focus on opportunities and to propose plans.

331 Help staff learn from their poor decisions. Train and encourage; don't criticize and blame.

332 When you make a wrong decision yourself, admit your mistake, correct it and learn from the experience.

Often decisions prove unsuccessful not because they are wrong but because the person making them is not sufficiently committed to them. Sell your decisions enthusiastically and you will contribute greatly to their success.

Personal Action Plan

Making decisions

Action	Target date	Achieved

9

How to delegate

The most important people-management skills are selecting the right people, training them hard, and delegating as much as possible.

When you read the trade and financial press (and even the political and sports pages), remind yourself that every top manager achieved their position in the same way: by demonstrating how to achieve results through others.

If you have a burning desire to do everything yourself, perhaps because you believe that no one can perform as well as you, forget for ever being a successful manager and resolve to spend the rest of your working life as a valuable subordinate, helping other managers on their way to the top.

But if you become a skilful delegator you will be a successful manager. Like all the other skills, delegation is not complicated – it involves some simple rules. In this book you have already been introduced to many, but they have been brought together here. Study and apply them.

333 Don't be proud of working excessively long hours or not taking your full holiday entitlement. You won't become a captain of industry with a nine-to-five attitude, but don't boast about working an 80-hour week.

Achieving the right balance between career and home is a personal matter. Some achieve that balance; many do not.

The young director of a pharmaceutical company who, because of pressure at work, had not seen his four-year-old daughter awake for three weeks, was pleased to find ways of saving 18 hours a week. He's now a better husband, father and company director.

334 Delegate to speed up the flow or work and to relieve pressure. Be prepared to pitch in yourself in emergencies, which should be rare.

335 Be pleased that members of your team are better at their jobs than you would be. Make the talents of individuals work for everyone's benefit.

336 Remember that a common reason for staff turnover is people being under-employed. Make jobs challenging – staff should be fully occupied. When you delegate everyone benefits:

- *You*, by having more time to do what you should be doing and enhancing your career prospects.
- *Your team*, because their work becomes more interesting and challenging.
- *Your company*, which achieves better value from you and your team.
- *Your customers*, who are served by a more efficient organization.
- *Your family*, who see more of you.

There are no losers.

337 If tasks you have delegated go wrong, you are still accountable. This means delegating well, not avoiding delegation.

338 Don't allow your staff to delegate upwards. When people bring you a problem they must also bring answers. They must satisfy you that they have thought the matter through, considered the options available, and decided which is best. Make it clear that you are always happy to listen but that you want people to make their own decisions.

339 Update job descriptions as you expand job content. Each member of your team must accept as many tasks as they can manage and then be trained to manage more. As you pass responsibility down, remember to inform any others who need to know.

340 Explain to managers who report to you that you expect work to be carried out at the most junior level possible. Don't expect the managers themselves to do work you delegate to them.

What and when

Your career will make a significant move forward when you accept the need to delegate more. But you must delegate appropriately.

341 Delegate as much and as often as possible. This will depend on your level in the organization. As a senior executive you should spend at least 90 per cent of your time managing – planning, organizing, controlling and providing leadership. As a first-line supervisor a more realistic mix might be 60 per cent doing and 40 per cent managing.

342 Delegate not as an exception but as a rule. As work comes down through the organization to you your first thought should be, 'Is there any reason for not delegating the work?' And second, 'To whom shall I delegate it?'

Do not delegate:

- Functions that company policy lays down that you must carry out – perhaps authorizing expenses claims, or being the keyholder.
- Personnel matters – selecting, appraising, disciplining, counselling, handling grievances of your immediate reports.
- Confidential matters – but there should be very few secrets.

343 When you are away, ensure continuity by making it clear who is responsible for what. Inform any others who need to know.

To whom

Your staff have different qualities and aptitudes. They each have the potential to make a greater contribution.

344 Delegate only to your immediate staff and ask your own manager not to delegate to your team.

345 As a rule delegate to an individual, not to a group. It is practically impossible to hold a group accountable except in the case of self-directed teams: with collective responsibility, 'to speak to one is to speak to all'.

346 Don't delegate only to high-flyers. You will be underestimating others – find out enough about each member of your team to know how much responsibility they can handle.

Some capable and ambitious people are naturally reserved – identify their potential and don't make them leave to achieve recognition elsewhere. The low proportion of women in management, even now, is due partly to many women being non-assertive and their managers not recognizing their potential.

347 Reassure people who doubt their ability, and increase their responsibility gradually, but don't bully people into taking on bigger jobs. Many talented people choose to operate well within their capabilities, and when someone has made a conscious decision it is unfair to impose your own preferences.

348 Give the team plenty of challenge and stretch them. If they are under unreasonable pressure seek more efficient methods before asking for more staff. The answer is not for you to do their work.

349 Don't block the careers of capable staff to make your own life easier. You are storing up trouble as talented people see less worthy people overtaking them.

350 Aim to train your own successor but do not promise promotion. If you believe there is no one who could do your job, think again. Could you do your manager's job? You almost certainly could, especially if you have been groomed for it. So it's likely that at least one member of your team could do your job – which will make it easier for the company to promote you.

How

Too often delegation is unsuccessful, usually because it is rushed. The transition should be gradual. Methods that you have been developing for years cannot be mastered in a few weeks.

351 When you delegate, ensure that your staff know exactly what you expect of them. As always, agree measurable performance targets and limits of authority. Don't rush briefing meetings – ask the person to summarize just to be sure.

352 Empower people to do the job. The delegation cannot work if the person has to come back repeatedly, asking for permission to proceed.

353 *Ask* people to do things rather than tell them.

354 Don't use the excuse 'it's quicker to do it myself'. If the job has to be done regularly this cannot be true.

Time spent training staff to carry out additional tasks is well invested. Think of a relay race where the baton should not slow down: both runners are running flat out at the moment of handover. After the safe transfer, the first runner (that's you) can turn your attention to something else while still checking that the race is won.

Following up

Don't be surprised if the person to whom you have delegated a task makes a few mistakes or needs reassurance. Be available.

If the person is a slow learner it doesn't necessarily mean that he/she is unsuitable.

355 Keep yourself informed on progress but don't crowd people. Taper off the training.

356 If problems arise, help people discover how to solve them rather than come to the rescue.

357 Review temporary assignments to reinforce experience and let the person practise what they have learnt.

358 Congratulate individuals publicly on a job well done.

359 Having completed the handover, resist the temptation to interfere. Allow people to develop their own methods as long as standards are maintained.

To reach the top you must master the art of delegation. Many able managers fail to achieve their potential because of their reluctance to pass work down the line.

Delegation is difficult because it means handing over tasks that you are good at and like doing. There is security in tasks you know, but as you master new skills and rise to greater challenges you will enjoy those too.

Personal Action Plan

Delegating

Action	Target date	Achieved

10

How to lead and motivate

More nonsense is spoken and written about leadership than any other management skill. Leadership is no more mysterious than the rest.

In all jobs, competence grows into confidence; leadership is no different. Some people might appear to be natural leaders but it is always because they have mastered their job and have a strength of purpose which attracts support. Charisma is not an innate quality. It is a blend of enthusiasm, determination to achieve a clearly defined goal and powerful communicating skills.

Communicating with groups comes more naturally to managers with outgoing personalities, but people who are more reserved can also learn the skill. Enthusiasm – a prerequisite of leadership – doesn't have to be very animated. Many captains of industry radiate a quiet confidence and resolve which excites those around them.

Don't confuse lack of assertiveness with a reserved nature. All good leaders are assertive but some are still quite shy.

Conditioning at home and at school will have caused all of us to regard ourselves either as leaders or subordinates. Unhelpful conditioning can be overcome when you understand leadership.

Different managers seem to excel in different situations. Some are at their best when driving a rapidly expanding business while others thrive on rescuing companies from collapse. But this is largely a question of appetite. Effective leaders know how to adapt their style to match changing circumstances.

List six leaders you admire and their qualities:

Leaders   **Qualities**

1.

2.

3.

4.

5.

6.

Now go through the list of qualities. Is there anything in the list that you can't develop? Add the qualities to your personal action plan and work at them. So leadership is not innate, it is acquired.

360 Give inexperienced people close attention. As they become more proficient, change to a hands-off style and enable them to develop their own methods. Give plenty of support and encouragement as they learn to be less dependent on you.

Very experienced people need freedom, and will resent close supervision. Walter Matthau said, 'My favourite director is Jack Lemmon. When we first worked together I said, "You're not going to teach me to act, are you?" We need to speak very little.'

361 Don't feel threatened by members of your team who demonstrate leadership ability. Harness their initiative and build on it.

362 Set a good example. Look purposeful and confident. If you let nervousness show, people will detect weakness and take advantage. People who worry most about street crime are often picked out as victims.

363 Stay fit. Weigh yourself regularly and exercise for enjoyment and health. Eat sensibly – people often gain weight when they lose confidence.

Your team should feel proud when you represent them in management meetings or visit other companies, so dress well.

364 Be polite. Say 'please' and 'thank you' but don't overdo it. Say 'no' politely but firmly, and if your first refusal is ignored persist: 'I do understand, Mary; however...'

365 Concentrate on effectiveness, not on being popular. Don't be reluctant to express anger, but don't lose self-control. Admit to yourself how you feel, then decide when to speak to the person involved, and make your point calmly. 'Mike, I feel very angry about what's happened...'

Don't agree with colleagues to avoid trouble. Disagree agreeably. Stay relaxed, allow the person to make their point, consider it carefully, then look for a solution.

Make it clear you're not being contentious: 'I wish I could go all the way with you on this, Romesh, but...'

Show that you appreciate others' views: 'I know that's the logical solution, but I think we need a more imaginative approach this time...' Or, agree in part: 'I agree we need to improve the delivery service, Sam, but a courier firm isn't the answer...'

366 If you are unhappy about something, be straightforward: 'Tony, there are two serious mistakes in this report: in future you must check your work carefully before giving it to me.' Don't sigh or sulk or behave moodily. But don't smile too much – it can suggest fear and uncertainty.

367 Promote pride in the company and its products. Help everyone understand the importance of their work and how they've each contributed to company success.

368 Remind your team that they must provide customer satisfaction – their own and the company's future depends on it. Stress the importance of retaining customers that they and other departments have worked hard to win. Encourage a healthy respect for competitors but emphasize the advantages your company offers.

369 Insist on 'zero defects'. Everyone must understand that near success simply isn't good enough. These high standards apply whether we are supplying internal or external customers.

370 Communicate face to face whenever possible. When you meet people, restrict pleasantries to one minute, or ten seconds on the telephone. At the first meeting decide whether to shake hands; try to avoid a misunderstanding. Give a firm handshake, but don't grip too long or pump too hard.

Never avoid eye contact – when people look at you, look back. You'll appear suspicious if you don't. Reinforce important points with a steady gaze.

By asking questions, you can keep conversations focused on what you need to discuss and avoid wasting expensive time.

Team leadership

Your team is more than a group of individuals. Under your leadership the team will develop an identity.

371 Encourage your team by looking proud and walking purposefully. Height is an advantage, but don't worry if you are short. Your bearing will underline your seniority.

372 Draw your team together by concentrating their attention on team targets. Improve team work by reminding people that as well as doing their own work they must support each other. Without shared aims, teams disintegrate.

373 Help your team feel interdependent. Give them a clear understanding of each other's responsibilities.

374 When you talk with your staff, talk about 'us/we/our'.

375 Bring the team together regularly for team briefings. Review progress and agree plans. Consider meetings you run and how your people typically behave. Some almost always behave positively; others seem to behave negatively.

Positive behaviour means making supportive comments, introducing new ideas, and solidifying information already available, building, 'I've thought of some more ideas on making Richard's plan work' and bringing in, 'Let's see what Amita has prepared.'

Negative contributors are people who constantly disagree, complain and criticize others in the team. Discover why they are so unhelpful and counterproductive. Are there rivalries? Do they feel undervalued – are you giving them full credit for their achievements?

376 Involve people, and don't dictate to your team. Talk *with* them, not *at* them. Encourage suggestions – expect at least one good idea a month from each team member.

377 Encourage loyalty to the company, not just to yourself, even when other staff are critical. Ask yourself if you are consistently loyal to your manager. Question his/her decisions in private meetings and express your views powerfully but put your energy into making decisions work, not proving they won't if you can't get them changed.

378 Give credit at team meetings to people who have performed especially well, but don't have favourites. Remember to thank support staff and to tell your manager about their progress.

379 Don't confide in team members. Everyone has a best friend! Even in the most open-style companies there are certain matters which you cannot disclose.

380 When there are difficulties between team members act quickly, before the situation deteriorates. Bring people together and talk things through.

381 Keep the working atmosphere pleasant by setting the right tone: work hard but don't be intense. Don't look anxious. The team will be enthused by a relaxed, confident approach.

382 Use the strengths of individuals to benefit the team. Philips, Volvo, Carlsberg Tetley and many other top companies have introduced 'team-building' concepts into manufacturing by bringing skilled people together and allowing the role of team leader to pass naturally to the person with the relevant expertise and knowledge.

Product quality and job satisfaction increase and absenteeism falls, but careful control is needed to avoid a reduction in productivity. Attractive incentives can be financed by savings on quality control.

383 Identify weaknesses in the team and tackle them quickly and decisively. Counsel and train hard, but when it becomes clear that people are unsuitable, they must go.

384 Pitch in when the team is under extreme pressure but be sure to identify crises caused by inefficiency or lack of effort.

Invite each team member to rank the following motivators:

- Money
- Recognition
- Achievement
- Security
- Working conditions
- Relationships/involvement
- Opportunity for advancement.

Then talk through the list with them and discuss how they might derive even greater satisfaction from their work.

385 When people leave the company, don't accuse them of being disloyal. Consider why they've decided to go.

386 If you socialize with people from work, behave responsibly. Your team are always watching you. If you feel uncomfortable socializing with colleagues and staff don't attempt to, and don't feel guilty.

Motivating individuals

Motivation means helping people achieve personal fulfilment. Your challenge is to help each team member find what they need from their work.

387 Make time to talk to people individually. Use positive 'body language' to encourage junior and senior members of your team to discuss their work. Listen assertively by looking at the other person. If you need to, make notes openly, then summarize action that you've agreed.

388 Learn the technique of closing conversations: 'Right then, Bill [rising from your seat], thanks for coming. I think that's as far as we can go today. Let's get together on the 28th to review progress.'

389 Don't become remote or detached from any of your staff – treat everyone with respect, whatever their status. Team members should be relaxed and natural in your presence.

Open conversations with people from other parts of the organization you recognize but haven't spoken to. They will be grateful when you take the initiative and any awkwardness will dissolve.

390 Reassure worriers and harness the enthusiasm of more confident team members. Remind people of their strengths and help them to develop their abilities through delegation and training.

Only praise when it is deserved. You'll seem patronizing or insincere if you congratulate people too often.

391 In meetings don't allow enthusiastic people to waste your time. Control talkative team members with closed questions: 'So you think we should go ahead, Christine?' or by interrupting: 'Nick, I appreciate how strongly you feel, but let's hear another opinion. Hassan, what's your view?'

392 Encourage your team. They must have high expectations of themselves and see difficulties as opportunities, not problems. Emphasize the benefits to them. They will be happier to do what you suggest: 'Sally, with two people away this week, you can prove to me that you're ready for promotion.'

393 Discuss performance day to day and at regular interviews. Before criticizing poor performance it might be appropriate to mention your satisfaction with other aspects of their work.

394 Deal with unsatisfactory behaviour assertively, not aggressively. When you discipline or counsel a member of your team, make it clear that you don't dislike them. It isn't a matter of personalities. Your criticisms mustn't be personal; your aim is to change their behaviour. Ask questions that invite agreement to help the person understand the problem: 'Jenny, do you agree that when we make a promise to a customer it's very important to keep it?' Never use sarcasm.

395 Show you are determined to see an improvement by following their progress closely and supportively.
   Only contact staff at home if it is unavoidable.

Financial and other rewards

Although financial reward is important, money alone is never reward enough.

396 Reward people by recognition, responsibility and status as well as financially. Encourage your staff to apply for promotion. Never feel threatened by their achievements – and try to fill senior vacancies from within your team.

397 Offer easily understood incentives to reward performance at all levels and in all departments, not only in sales. Increased earnings for achieving profit, production, quality and efficiency targets benefit the company and the individual.

398 Design attractive schemes that unite rather than divide your team. At Invicta a promise of a two-day break at a smart country club if a difficult sales target was achieved generated even greater efforts than usual. We reached the target and enjoyed two days relaxing together.

399 Make your pay policy competitive, fair and generous to high achievers. Relocation expenses, company cars, private health insurance and a good pension scheme are investments, not costs.

Employee share schemes will also motivate staff and encourage long-term commitment.

Your leadership style

Don't confuse assertiveness with aggression. If you impose your own rights and needs at the expense of people around you, you are being aggressive. Assertive managers push hard to achieve goals but without violating the rights and needs of their team.

If you are inclined to be aggressive, or submissive, you can become more assertive. Start to operate assertively and a successful management style will follow.

400 Control space and learn to feel comfortable on other people's 'territory'. Move in a smooth, relaxed way – if you rush, people think there is a crisis.

Enter meeting rooms confidently. Pick a prominent central seat and head for it purposefully. Take charge if people are uncomfortable. Say 'if no one minds I'll turn up the air conditioning', walking to the dial as you speak. Behave naturally whoever you are with. Call people by their name, not 'Sir' or 'Madam'.

401 Be a good ambassador. Outside work speak well of the company and your team.

402 When you make a mistake don't pretend to be infallible; admit you were wrong. Respond positively to fair criticism. It isn't a personal attack, so listen to everything people say and promise an improvement.

Encourage your team to receive constructive criticism and to be assertive when dealing with each other.

403 When there's a problem stay calm. Take control, tackle the problem systematically and don't panic.

404 Don't generate anxiety – you must concentrate on positive attitudes. Nervous habits like smoking and drinking heavily will discourage your staff. You don't need 'comfort tricks' to be a successful manager.

Be aware of nervous mannerisms. If close friends tell you that you repeat yourself, or put your hand over your mouth, or play with your hair, then welcome their comments and break the habits. Signs of stress can spread to your staff.

405 Encourage good relationships with other departments. Consider whether you have enough contact with other managers.

Fifty years or so ago, studies of leadership concentrated on the personal qualities of effective leaders, like self-confidence, determination and enthusiasm. It was widely believed that these were unchangeable personality traits and therefore those lacking any one of them were not suitable material. As our understanding has improved, we have learned that good leaders succeed because they do certain things, and personality, far from being fixed, does change. If you put this advice into practice you will be the kind of leader everyone wants to work for.

Personal Action Plan

Leadership and motivation

Action	Target date	Achieved

11

How to communicate

Communicate upwards, sideways and with your team all the time – not just when there's a problem. Don't imitate a very large computer company which, when it hit hard times, issued regular bulletins with full details of how bad the situation was but started to withhold figures again when trading improved.

Don't tell your staff any less than you tell shareholders; both have a stake in the business. 'To be a manager is to be a communicator. The person and the function are inextricably interwoven' (Morris E. Massey).

Communication means sending and receiving messages so that others understand what's on your mind and you understand what is on theirs.

406 Be sincere and direct. Dropping hints or being sarcastic is indirect and non-assertive. Say clearly what you want to say, avoid colloquialisms or jargon unless you are sure you'll be understood.

STD might mean Subscriber Trunk Dialling, Sexually Transmitted Disease or Select, Train, Delegate. Any misunderstanding could be embarrassing. Use familiar rather than obscure words, and spell out ambiguous abbreviations.

407 Have a good dictionary to hand and increase your vocabulary by looking up words that are new to you. Keep a notebook of new words with their meanings.

408 Persuade by seeing situations from the other person's point of view and explaining the benefits to them of accepting your ideas.

409 Let your enthusiasm show. It's not a false display – it's an honest expression of deeply held beliefs. When Richard Branson speaks of Virgin and its products he wins people over by being a committed manager. There is only one thing more contagious than enthusiasm and that is the lack of it.

410 Don't speak too loudly or raise your voice in anger. Bullying won't make your views any more persuasive – logic is far more powerful.

411 Don't say or write anything intending to hurt people. It cannot be withdrawn, however much you regret it later. You don't have to like people to work with them, but try to build bridges rather than make enemies.

412 Don't exaggerate for effect. Other people will assume that you always overstate, and make allowance. It is far more impressive to understate when solving customer problems, to under-promise and then over-deliver.

Face to face

In recent years, communication methods have become even more sophisticated, but still none is more important than face-to-face communication.

413 Don't try to disguise your accent, but do speak clearly. If you are with people who might have difficulty understanding you, slow down and watch their eyes for signs of uncertainty, checking if they haven't understood.

414 Don't use 'um' and 'er' or meaningless phrases like 'you know', basically', 'in actual fact'. They are unnecessary space fillers and detract from your message.

415 Practise conversation skills. Call people by their name, ask questions, show interest, listen attentively and develop techniques for bringing conversations to a close: 'Thanks again, Jim. I've enjoyed our meeting. I'll see you on Tuesday at 2 pm.'

416 Don't interrupt unless the other person is digressing. If someone's speech is slow or hesitant don't finish sentences for them, mouth what they are saying or prompt them; be patient.

417 Remember that it isn't only what you say that registers but how you say it. Don't use an abrasive tone and never talk down to junior people. Don't use a subservient tone when speaking with senior managers or with customers.

418 Record your voice, listen to it critically, and improve your diction, if necessary by practising tongue-twisters in front of a mirror.

419 If your voice is inclined to be monotonous, breathe deeply and concentrate on projecting it more powerfully. This will probably mean opening your mouth wider.

420 Maintain eye contact but don't stare people out. Research suggests that in conversation the more assertive person often disengages eye contact first, but after two or three seconds, and then slowly. When face to face don't try to look into both eyes simultaneously; you'll appear cross-eyed. Look into one eye and then into the other.

421 Don't speak too quickly. It suggests a lack of confidence.

422 Don't allow your voice to dip at the end of sentences. This gives the impression that you are bored or lack enthusiasm.

When making a statement don't allow your voice to go up as if you are asking a question – you will sound unsure.

423 When speaking with people don't be distracted by other things going on in the room. Give the conversation your full attention. If your eyes are flicking in other directions it is rude and unfair to the speaker.

424 Don't talk too much. Even when informing, allow the other person to speak for at least 20 per cent of the time. Obtain feedback to check understanding.

In other interviews or conversations do less than 50 per cent of the talking even when you are aiming to persuade.

425 Encourage people to talk about themselves. Acknowledge their expertise and draw on it: 'Tony, you're good at this, what do you think? 'You' is always better than 'I'.

Think of the most boring person you know: aren't they always talking about themselves?

426 Don't present your opinions as facts. Say 'It seems to me that…', not 'It is…'. Don't be reluctant to admit difficulty in making up your mind, but don't procrastinate or contemplate endlessly – you will appear indecisive.

427 Don't be serious all the time, or you will be very dull company. You don't have to tell jokes, but look for humour in day-to-day events and tell anecdotes to lighten conversations. Tell stories against yourself, and do not ridicule others.

428 Earn a reputation for being trustworthy with confidences, which includes refusing to be drawn into gossip.

Developing your listening skills

Most managers simply hear. You, on the other hand, will watch and listen.

429 Listen carefully to what people say, and particu- larly to inflections in their voice, which will often give you a better understanding of their attitude. Members of your team who mention a certain competitor with awe might need some training. Remind them of your company's relative strengths and how the competitor is vulnerable.

Observe people's body language, including facial expressions. It will often give clues as to a person's thoughts – respond with a question to explore uncertainty or disagreement.

430 Don't try to remember a large number of facts from a conversation or meeting. Most people have difficulty retaining more than seven separate points. Write them down and, if appropriate, invite the other person to confirm them.

Test your short-term memory by reading a newspaper article with nine or more facts, close the newspaper and five minutes later write down what you remember. In business there are many distractions, and mistakes can prove very costly.

Learn to make brief notes – or try using 'mind maps' (key words linked together visually to show how the ideas relate to one another).

431 Use non-verbal signals to affirm your interest and attention. Lean forward, assume an 'open' posture. Smile, nod, wince, frown and so on. When appropriate encourage with 'mm', 'yes', 'really?', 'go on', 'of course', but don't prompt. You might unwittingly lead the other person to express your point of view instead of their own.

Research shows that nodding will help people to open up and sometimes reveal more than they had intended.

432 If you don't understand, ask for clarification – never pretend to understand. But don't embarrass the other person. Say, 'I'm sorry, Julie, but could you go through that again, please?'

433 Summarize what the other person has said to check that you have understood. If you are engaged in a negotiation, summarize neutrally. 'So the situation is: you could deliver by the 19th if we confirm by the 14th, and your asking price is 6 per cent above our budget.'

434 Keep an open mind. Listen to everything a person says. Don't make assumptions – you could be wrong. Don't allow your concentration to wander if a person or subject is not particularly interesting to you, and don't let your mind move to what you are going to say next. Stay tuned in.

435 Don't be influenced by emotive words. Listen for illogical arguments: 'I'm determined', 'You're bombastic', 'He's inflexible' depends on your standpoint. One person's freedom fighter is another's terrorist.

Try to be objective. The more certain the speaker, the more guarded you should be. Beware of people who take extreme positions: the truth is seldom black or white.

Conducting meetings

Nothing in business is more excruciatingly painful than attending a badly run meeting. Follow the advice given here and people will look forward to attending your meetings.

436 Bring your team together at least once a month to inform, review progress, plan, consider new ideas and to engender team spirit. Allow people to put items on the agenda, which you should circulate in advance, giving managers an opportunity to consult their teams and come along with fully formed ideas.

437 Control meetings you chair firmly but without stifling. Work through the agenda briskly, keeping contributions brief and to the point. Don't insist on everyone speaking through the chair. If a discussion develops between two or three people, allow it to continue for as long as it is useful.

Only one person should speak at a time; don't allow splinter groups.

438 Prevent very talkative group members from monopolizing the meeting. Curtail their contributions by waiting for them to finish a point, disengaging eye contact and putting the question to another group member. However talkative a person is they will have to draw breath eventually – 'Yes, thanks Felipe. What do you think, Helen?'

439 Agree action minutes, including action to be taken, by whom and when after each item, then send everyone a copy immediately. Sometimes a photocopy of your hand-written minutes provided at the end of the meeting will be sufficient. Follow up to ensure that agreed action is taken and chase hard if there is any doubt.

440 Don't dominate meetings or impose your own views. If you are genuinely interested in obtaining the views of others, and you should be, invite them to tell you what they think first. Saying, 'I think we should introduce the XL model immediately. What do you say, John?' is unlikely to elicit an honest answer from an ambitious subordinate. 'When do you think we should launch the XL?' is better. Less confident staff are more willing to express doubts with their colleagues around them.

Divide-and-rule tactics are manipulative and unfair. You want resistance out in the open, so really listen to what is being said.

When a decision is made, sell it enthusiastically to the team. Emphasize the benefits, explain the logic and answer any doubts or fears honestly. Don't be angry with people who have misgivings – win them over.

441 Have decisions made democratically at meetings only if you are willing to be outvoted. Otherwise consult and then announce your decision, explain it but don't apologize for it. Your purpose is to make the right decisions and they are not always popular.

Speaking to groups

Many managers' legs turn to jelly when they have to stand up and address a large gathering.

Like other management skills, speaking to groups is a matter of observing a simple set of rules. No one is naturally a brilliant speaker. Even professionals admit to being nervous.

442 Don't allow nervousness to prevent you from addressing your team. It is an important part of your role as leader and you must learn to feel comfortable speaking on your feet. As you practise you will feel less nervous and be content to speak at larger gatherings. Stand for the part of each meeting when you present performance figures. You will find it easier and easier.

443 Plan with IPSQC. Introduction to gain the group's attention and interest, the **Presentation**

of your material in a logical sequence, **S**ummary covering the main points briefly again, invite **Q**uestions and end with a **C**onclusion, pointing the way ahead, ending on a high note, and sending the audience away 'fired up'.

444 Use cards for your notes. Postcards are ideal, and should be easily readable at arm's length. Use headings and a sequence of ideas under each, and number the cards in case you drop them.

Don't use a script unless you are very nervous, the group is extremely large or the function very formal (perhaps your speech will be reported in the media and using the wrong word could change the meaning of what you are trying to say).

445 Explain in your introduction the relevance of the subject to your audience, the sequence of the talk and whether they should ask questions during the talk or at the end. Tell them whether you will be giving out printed notes so that they know whether to make their own.

446 Always rehearse talks aloud, including the presentations that you make to colleagues on special occasions, like giving them wedding presents, long-service awards and so on. As your career progresses, 'saying a few words' will become a regular and enjoyable duty.

447 Don't let your speech overrun, especially if yours is one of a number of presentations at a conference or company meeting. It is more courteous to take up slightly less than your allocated time. Your rehearsal will tell you how much material to discard. To overcome gaps, you could send reading material in advance.

448 Use visuals to make the presentation more interesting and to express your message. If you are using videos or 35 mm slides have them made professionally. People are accustomed to high standards and anything less will detract from the presentation.

449 Don't put your notes on a table and lean over them – your voice will be directed downwards and you will restrict your breathing. Use a table-top lectern. Many speakers don't know what to do with their hands. Don't put them in your pockets, behind your back or cross your arms. The lectern is the answer: hold on to it gently with both hands. As your confidence grows you will begin to use gestures naturally to support what you are saying.

450 Project your voice to fill the room but don't shout. Assume that someone in the back row is slightly hard of hearing – they must hear every word. Keep your head up, breathe at punctuation marks and don't rush.

Use silences to emphasize points of particular importance. Watch expert orators. You might not agree with their views but you can learn from their technique.

451 Don't rehearse hand movements. If they are not spontaneous they look odd. If you are not naturally animated, use your voice and visuals for emphasis.

452 Make eye contact with as many members of the group as possible. Beware of homing in on a person who is showing tremendous enthusiasm for what you are saying. Don't move your eyes from person to person in a set pattern – let them focus on people in any order for two or three seconds. This is possible even with huge gatherings. The last time you saw a big star live on stage didn't you feel him or her make eye contact with you? Don't overlook people who are sitting closest to you.

453 If you use a flipchart, stand it to your left if you are right-handed, and if you are not experienced at using one, practise. Use large writing, simple illustrations and colour to add interest.

Powerpoint or an overhead projector will enable you to show images on a screen, which is especially useful when addressing large groups. Don't point up at the screen. Point at the slide and retain eye contact with your audience.

454 If you are showing 35 mm slides, ask a colleague to operate the projector, or, if possible, use a remote control. Whatever types of projector you use, focus them in advance and have spare bulbs at hand.

455 Pay careful attention to your appearance. If you look good you will feel more confident and impress the audience. This is always important, but especially so if it is your own team you are addressing.

456 Bring your speeches to a close, thank your audience for their attention and sit down unhesitatingly. Even when making an impromptu speech, perhaps to propose a vote of thanks, don't ramble or talk until you run out of ideas. Keep it brief and to the point. The last impression is the lasting impression.

Written communication

The pen may be mightier than the sword but the written word remains the least effective form of communication.

Weak managers write countless letters and memoranda and communicate by e-mail or fax, preferring to correspond rather than deal with others person to person.

As an assertive manager you should establish contact face to face or by telephone whenever possible, but you also need to be skilful at expressing yourself in writing.

457 Use written communication to save time or money or when the matter has to be put on record. Keep it brief – usually no more than one page.

458 Answer correspondence within one working day or, if you can't obtain the necessary information, acknowledge receipt of the communication immediately and follow up as quickly as possible: 'Thank you for your letter dated 6 June. I am sure you understand that it will take a day or two to carry out a detailed search of our records. I will give you the information you require before the weekend. Thank you for your cooperation and please let me know if I can help in any way in the meantime.'

459 Write to confirm arrangements: 'I enjoyed our meeting on Tuesday and I am writing to confirm what we agreed. I will arrange for … You will be sending … We will meet again at your office in Newtown on Wednesday 13 June when I will be joined by our legal adviser Pauline Nisbett.'

460 Write to say thank you or well done: 'Jim, I have just seen the October sales figures. Congratulations to you and your colleagues for exceeding the target by 17 per cent. I realize how much hard work you have all put in. To have won the Excelsior contract in the face of such stiff competition from both Albion and Zeta must be worth a mention in the trade press. I have asked Sunbeam

Photography to telephone you to arrange a convenient time for a team photograph.'

461 Make a preliminary list of points you want to cover and plan your e-mail or letter as you would a speech. It must have: a beginning, an introduction to identify the subject and perhaps a heading; a middle with your message in a logical sequence (a new paragraph for each item, numbered if appropriate); and an end, pointing ahead to what is to happen next.

Follow convention in signing off, using 'yours faithfully' or 'yours sincerely'.

462 Use short sentences and a natural style. Use punctuation to help the reader understand your message. Read through your draft and delete unnecessary words and phrases. Never use a pedantic or puffed-up style to impress – you will only confuse the reader. Keep your correspondence as simple as possible.

463 Dictate only if you are fluent; otherwise you will waste time correcting mistakes. This will cause frustration and unnecessary expense.

Learn to touch-type and improve your speed so that you can type your own brief memos and reports.

464 Ensure that your letters, faxes, e-mails and memos create a favourable impression. Check for spelling or grammatical mistakes before you sign. Avoid using the same word repeatedly. Buy a Roget's *Thesaurus* to complement your dictionary so that you can always use the right word.

465 If you are unable to sign personally, do not allow others to pp your signature without an explanation: 'Dictated by Janet Jones and signed in her absence.'

466 Develop your written style by reading a quality newspaper and well written literature. Avoid out-of-date terms like 'of even date', '17th inst.', 'the writer...', 'I remain'. They will give an old-fashioned impression of you and your organization.

467 Have longer letters and reports typed by a skilful typist. You are being judged even before the envelope is opened. The presentation and layout are part of the message, and anything short of perfection will damage your reputation.

468 Written reports can be very boring but yours mustn't be. Use an unpretentious style and, when possible, illustrations to add interest and enhance the message.

Your purpose is to inform and probably to persuade. The reader, probably your manager, is a busy person so don't make him/her read the entire document. Present your proposals towards the beginning and support them with the evidence, which might need to be contained in appendices.

469 Make your reports visually appealing. Put them in an attractive folder, with a title page, an index, and set out your terms of reference. Use different typestyles and graphics to highlight important points.

Make data interesting. Do not show columns of figures: graphs, bar charts and pie charts are more appealing and easier to understand. Present facts honestly.. Never distort or omit information you find inconvenient – take a fair and balanced view.

Using the telephone

The spoken word, but without vision. The telephone requires particular skills.

470 Set your team a good example by always answering your telephone before the third ring, and greet the caller in a businesslike way: 'Good morning, Jim Tullis.'

471 Begin to talk business immediately and don't engage in small talk. By saying, 'How's the weather where you are?', 'What did you do at the weekend?', you are wasting the company's money on an unnecessarily long call and failing to give value for money for your time. You are also setting a bad example to your department. Imagine the annual cost of everyone wasting the first couple of minutes of every telephone call.

472 Listen and let the caller know you are listening with the vocal equivalent of nods, frowns and smiles: 'yes', 'right', 'I see', and keep a note pad beside your telephone.

473 Speak at the same volume as you would face to face. Don't shout or whisper, hold the handset properly and speak directly into the mouthpiece.

474 At the end of the conversation summarize what action is to be taken and thank the person for calling – don't slam down the receiver.

475 Plan outgoing calls by listing the points you want to discuss, gathering any relevant information you might need.

476 Allow the person you contact to introduce themselves. Don't assume it is your contact, then headline your call as you would a letter: 'Helen, it's about the Amalgamated contract.'

477 Keep conversations to the point. If the other person digresses, tactfully bring them back to the subject. If you have to look something up explain that you will be only a few minutes. If it is going to take longer, arrange to call back.

478 Read the user's manual for your telephone system and make full use of it. Let the instrument redial while you do something else; use the conferencing facility instead of calling a meeting. Let the telephone remember the numbers you often need.

479 Cover the mouthpiece if you have to talk to someone else in the office and remember that the caller can probably still hear you.

480 Don't chew, smoke or slouch when on the telephone. Treat the conversation as a normal meeting and smile as you would face to face.

481 If you let someone down, telephone immediately to apologize – don't wait for them to complain. Give them as much notice of the problem as possible. Perhaps you can work out a solution together and avoid damaging the relationship.

482 Be as assertive on the telephone as you are face to face, but without non-verbal signals it is what you say and how you say it that must convey the right impression.

Don't use an aggressive or submissive tone, and don't be put off by the lack of visual feedback: ask questions to test reactions. If people telephone when it is inconvenient tell them so politely, and call them back. This includes your manager.

483 If you are going to be away from your desk, arrange for someone to take your calls – a continuously ringing telephone advertises a lack of personal organization. Return calls immediately.

484 Emphasize to your team the importance of using the telephone professionally, and train them. Use recorded role plays to give practice in handling difficult situations. Advise people with monotonous voices to breathe more deeply and vary their tone.

485 Explain the need to take advantage of off-peak reduced rates. If a telephone call can wait, the other person might even call first. Of course, urgent matters must be attended to immediately.

Emulate people around you who impress you with their communication skills. A very limited vocabulary is a common failing – most people restrict themselves to about two thousand words, which makes it difficult for them to express shades of meaning.

Build up your vocabulary and you will develop a skill which is a prerequisite for those bound for the top – mastery of the spoken and written word.

Personal Action Plan

Communicating

Action	Target date	Achieved

12

How to manage your career

You have considered ways of developing your effectiveness and, if you fulfil your action plans your results will put you in the running for promotion.

In a perfect world your manager would be helping you prepare for the next step of your career, but often you will be left on your own to cope as best you can.

486 Prove your suitability for promotion by delegating – achieving results through others. If you are struggling to do your present job, you're not promotable. The diagram on page 162 shows why delegation is vital if your aim is to reach the top.

On being promoted

Promotion means change, challenge and excitement, but

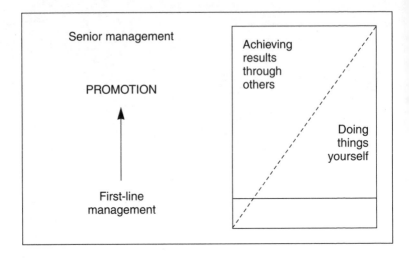

also some anxiety. This applies equally to a move into first-line management or on to the board.

487 If you are promoted from within the team, first let go of your old job. If you cling on to jobs you like doing and don't trust others to do, it's bad for you (you'll be working 70 to 80 hours a week), bad for your staff (they've got a part-time manager who underestimates them), and bad for the company (which isn't getting value for money from your salary increase).

Fill the vacancy or study the job description and decide to whom you'll delegate each area of responsibility.

488 When you come into a management position from outside the company, use the early weeks (months in a very senior post) to learn and benefit from your ability to look at the department almost as an outsider – how the telephone is answered, the appearance of the shop through the customer's eyes, and so on. You will lose this advantage as familiarity grows.

489 If possible, talk to your predecessor about the job. Concentrate on facts – your predecessor might be biased.

490 Review the department's recent performance. If it is performing well, aim to build on that success. If business has been going badly, you have a more exciting challenge: to turn it round.

491 Call your people together soon after your promotion and talk to them as a team. Tell them about yourself and your style of management. Tell them about the high standards you expect and that you're looking forward to working with them.

492 Make it clear how you want the relationship to work. The trend today is towards first names and a relaxed, informal style, but some organizations still encourage a formal approach.

You must choose the style that you feel most comfortable with, but don't assume that respect will come with formality. Respect has to be earned – it does not come automatically with rank. The only way to win respect is to give it.

Most successful managers do not want the kind of subservience that was considered normal 30 years ago, when managers had different car parks, eating places and toilet facilities from those of their staff.

If you have an office, operate an open-door policy but ask people to make appointments if they want ten minutes or more of your time.

493 Have a one-to-one meeting with each team member. Invite them to tell you about themselves but talk mainly about their work.

If you've been promoted from within the team, you need to establish a new relationship. It's up to you to take the initiative and build trust and understanding. Never cut yourself off from people because you've been promoted.

494 Counsel anyone who thinks they should have been promoted into the position. Ideally, your manager will have explained to them why they have not been selected this time, but this rarely happens.

Tell the person that you understand their disappointment and hope they'll be successful in future. But you need their support now and expect full cooperation.

This tactic succeeds nine times out of ten. When it doesn't, the counselling approach gives way to discipline. Talk the matter through again – but never in public.

Don't be angry, but show your disappointment: 'You're being uncooperative and I'm not happy about it. I'm not receiving the support you promised.'

Make it clear that unless they change their attitude, their behaviour will almost certainly jeopardize their future promotion prospects – jealousy and unhelpfulness are not management qualities. Seek their commitment to improve – then shake hands.

If the person is still uncooperative, continue the disciplinary procedure to a conclusion. With luck, there will be a change of attitude; otherwise dismissal becomes inevitable.

Never ignore someone who is uncooperative. The rest of your team will want decisive action to solve the problem.

495 Remember that *everyone* takes time to adapt to a change of manager. Your staff will be hoping that you're the type of manager they want to work for. Keep in close contact during this honeymoon period by 'walking the job' and giving the right signals.

496 Don't be anxious about managing people who are older than you. You have been promoted because of your suitability, not your age. Don't think that someone your parents' age resents working for you – they might not want the responsibilities that come with promotion.

Older people will respect you if you ask them for advice and use their experience to help the team.

497 Learn about existing systems and make changes only after careful consideration. Put together a plan and talk it through with your manager.

498 Don't be timid about asking people, especially your staff, to explain points. Don't imagine that senior people must appear to know everything.

499 Keep in touch with your manager. If you are worried, he/she will reassure you. It's natural to feel anxious on being promoted, but don't let your anxiety show or your team, too, will become anxious.

Your manager will remind you that you have the credentials and that you will be given training to help you master your new job. The company doesn't expect you to be fully effective immediately.

If your manager seems too busy to help, explain that you need support and arrange a regular meeting. If there has been no mention of training, devise a training plan for yourself and initiate it. If you don't have the authority, ask for approval.

If you are unclear about certain aspects of your job, prepare a draft job description including standards and limits of authority and meet to talk it through. Don't waste your manager's time by going empty-handed.

500 Communicate with your team. Consider holding weekly briefings. If everyone fully understands their role and the company's aims, there'll be no need for a grapevine – a cancer within the business.

When managers don't communicate, rumours spread. The grapevine only reacts to bad news and then makes it worse. It's unfair for your people to hear rumours of redundancies and pay cuts.

Be honest and open at these meetings – give good and bad news. When you have bad news, tell people what they need to do to improve the situation and send them back to work feeling enthusiastic.

Twelve hundred people work at Scottish Widows' Head Office in Edinburgh. Once a month on a Wednesday morning senior managers meet and briefings are passed down through the organization. By Friday, over a thousand people are fully informed – from a reliable source.

In a survey for *The Director* magazine, four out of five firms which improved communications also reported improved morale and loyalty.

501 Set a good example – your team reflect you. Don't operate double standards. If you dress untidily and you're often late, you can't complain about their personal appearance and bad timekeeping.

502 Don't shut yourself away – circulate from day one. Managers used to sit in their offices at a big desk behind a big door, communicating through memos and by summoning people to them. To be effective you need to be visible.

Find a reason for visiting staff. As you begin to circulate you have more reason to see them. Follow through people's ideas – act on them and keep the person informed; if you can't adopt their suggestion, tell them why.

503 Feel comfortable with your seniority. Remind yourself that you are the manager by right. Your team should feel proud of you and the way you represent them. Achieve this by: the way you look – look good and you'll feel good; your dress, grooming, bearing, the way you walk with a purpose; the way you communicate – look people in the eye when speaking with them. Express yourself fluently and confidently. Don't mumble or whisper – speak with conviction.

Communicate face to face whenever possible rather than by letter/memo/e-mail/notices. Ask questions and listen attentively.

504 Don't strive to be popular. Concentrate on being the type of manager you would like to work for: a strong leader, not one who ingratiates him/herself with the team.

Spend time 'at the sharp end'. If you are a production manager spend time on the shop floor; if you are a sales manager spend time out in the field.

Your team shouldn't behave differently when you walk into the room. If you're with them enough they'll behave naturally.

505 Be loyal 'up' and 'down' the company. The seniority that comes with promotion will test your loyalty. Weak managers can prove their boss wrong by openly criticizing their decisions. If you tell your people a new idea won't work, that becomes a self-fulfilling prophecy. Disloyalty is reflected by staff who run down the company, its products – and their manager.

Loyalty is earned by example. If you represent the company professionally to your department and represent your team when dealing with your manager, you'll be enhancing your chances of being promoted again – and again!

Developing your effectiveness

You will never stop learning. This book encapsulates the equivalent of 90000 years of experience, but is still only a foundation upon which to build.

506 Review your performance continuously. Spend 15 minutes at the end of each week considering your successes and mistakes, and learn from them.

507 Observe other managers and learn from them. Focus your attention on managers in your own organization at all levels, including junior managers.

Look particularly for good management techniques and adopt those you feel comfortable with.

508 Consider good and bad managers you have worked for, and good and bad school teachers. Remind yourself what the better managers did to bring out the best in you and resolve not to make the mistakes of the worst.

Read books on management. You will always learn something. Books on management are much more helpful now than 20 years ago when most were written by people with no managerial experience and were often based on theory which, when put to the test, didn't work.

Start a library at work and fill it with books written by and about successful managers and their organizations. Read the financial and trade press. Keep a knowledge file – a scrapbook of examples of successful management.

510 As you become more experienced, take a particular interest in helping junior managers to develop. As you teach them, you will remind yourself of the important principles.

Some companies use a method called 'mentoring' – young managers are adopted by senior managers from a different part of the organization. They go to them to talk things through as they would with a favourite aunt or uncle. Both benefit from the relationship.

511 Be determined to improve. Experience alone will not bring improvement.

Welcome constructive criticism. Invite it and don't automatically respond by defending yourself and making excuses. Just as it is easy for you to see other people's faults, so it is easy for others to notice yours.

512 Work hard – there is no easy way to the top. Assuming that nepotism isn't your route to success, only good results will advance your career. Don't look for short cuts. Expect to have to prove yourself every step of the way.

513 Be yourself – behave naturally, whoever you are with. Don't adopt a false accent or try to impress by being over-polite. The façade will be obvious to everyone and instead of impressing will show your lack of self-confidence.

514 Concentrate on being positive. Look around you at the least effective managers – notice how they grumble and moan. They pass on their negative attitudes to their staff, resulting in low morale, high absenteeism and rapid staff turnover, particularly of high-calibre people.

Focus attention on what has to be done, not what can't. And always present your ideas positively, concentrating more on answers than on problems.

515 Don't play politics. Undercover intrigue is indirect and weak. Be open and direct and don't gossip.

516 Learn at least one foreign language. As a senior manager you will travel overseas; fluency in Russian, Japanese or French will put you at an advantage over English-only speakers.

517 Don't be concerned with empire building. Your seniority is not measured by the number of people you have working for you – effective managers have tight staffing levels.

518 Set your senior managers a good example. Give them full support and meet often enough to operate as a close partnership.

Offer suggestions and demonstrate effective management techniques – they will be influenced by your success. The best way to open up your career opportunities is to cause your manager to be promoted.

Living longer

Stressed managers die early. You need to be successful *and* live long enough to enjoy the fruits of your labours.

519 Keep yourself fit. Exercise regularly and keep within your ideal weight. Use the stairs instead of the lift – try to walk at least two miles every day. Don't smoke, drink only in moderation and eat fewer animal fats.

Eat breakfast and lunch each day – an evening meal is less important. Have a thorough medical check-up periodically and follow your doctor's advice.

520 Don't fill your life with work. Interests and hobbies that totally absorb you will make you forget work. It's important to switch off – you will be fresher when you return to work.

521 Don't allow work to damage your marriage or family relationships. Of course, there will sometimes be a conflict but with luck both your company and your family are willing to be flexible.

Help your spouse and family appreciate the importance to you of building a successful career, but if the two parts of your life are incompatible, then you will have to think carefully and solve the problem.

522 Take your full holiday entitlement and encourage your team to do the same.

523 Develop your car-driving skills and never drive aggressively. If possible take the train – it's far less stressful.

Shaping your own destiny

Success is only a matter of luck: ask any failure!

524 Always look for ways of improving efficiency and profitability. Introduce change – don't resist it. As you become older, you must fight an inclination to cling to the past; management is concerned with creating the future.

525 Plan your career – occasionally doors swing open unexpectedly, but don't rely on that happening. Set yourself career targets and plan the route to achieve them.

Research in the US suggests that the careers of chief executive officers will almost always have included starting up an operation, perhaps a new branch or an overseas division, *and* rescuing an ailing branch/company from closedown.

Put yourself forward for assignments like these while others are shrinking back through fear of failure or pressure.

So now you have it; 90 000 years of experience to help accelerate your career. We and the 6000 managers who made this book possible wish you a long, successful and, most of all, an enjoyable career in management.

Personal Action Plan

Career

Action	Target date	Achieved